READING

IN THE MODERN INFANTS' SCHOOL

NORA L. GODDARD

Inspector of Infants' Education, I.L.E.A.
Formerly Headmistress, Henry Fawcett Infants' School, London

University of London Press Ltd

As the author is in the employ of the I.L.E.A.
it is necessary to state that the Authority accepts
no responsibility for the author's opinions.

SBN 340 09042 1 Boards
SBN 340 11844 x Unibook
First published 1958
Third edition copyright © 1969 Nora L. Goddard
Photographs copyright © 1969 University of London Press Ltd
Jacket photograph copyright © 1969 Henry Grant AIBP

University of London Press Ltd
St. Paul's House, Warwick Lane, London E.C.4

Printed in England by Elliott Bros & Yeoman Ltd., Liverpool

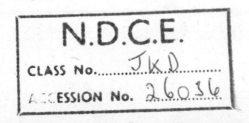

READING IN THE MODERN INFANTS' SCHOOL

CONTENTS

REVIEW OF SOME RECENT DEVELOPMENTS IN
THE TEACHING OF READING

(Preface to the Third Edition)

SINCE this book was published in 1958 there have been some important comments upon and investigations into the most effective ways of learning and teaching reading. Some sources of these comments are:

(a) *Reading in the Primary School*, an account of the National Foundation for Educational Research Survey, which was carried out in a sample of sixty Kent Primary schools (Newnes Educational Publishing Co. Ltd, 1959);

(b) *Reading in Infants' Classes*, an account of a further survey by the N.F.E.R., carried out in one hundred urban Infants' schools (N.F.E.R. in England and Wales, 1967);

(c) the research carried out by the Reading Research Unit of London University into the use of the Initial Teaching Alphabet as a medium for teaching reading. There were a number of interim reports, but the fullest account to date is *Evaluation of the Initial Teaching Alphabet*, 1967;

(d) *Children and their Primary Schools*, the report of the Central Advisory Council, which in its review of primary education in England makes many pertinent comments upon how reading is and might be taught. (H.M.S.O., 1967).

This chapter attempts to relate the findings of these enquiries to what was said in earlier editions of this book.

Two things stand out from these investigations. On the one hand there is among teachers an increasing awareness of reading as a part of a total learning situation. "The intense interest shown by young children in the world about them, their powers of concentration on whatever is occupying their attention or serving their immediate purposes, are apparent to both teachers and parents. Skills of reading and writing . . . can best be taught when the need for them is evident to children." (*Children and their Primary Schools*, paragraph 530). Combined with this is a growing tendency to provide a free and apparently unstructured daily programme. On the other hand, investigations have indicated that the teaching of reading still has to be regarded as a precise art. "One headmistress of an Infants' school . . . produced an excellent reading record. She streamed top infants for ability, and initiated a small class for backward readers. She gave children in this class a Terman–Merrill intelligence test and spent a long time trying to discover causes of difficulties in reading. She herself taught, helping the class teacher, initiating a scheme of work for the whole school but encouraging teachers to implement it imaginatively, implementing a systematic, almost formal, whole word approach in the reception class and soon getting children started on word-building. Pupils who were in the top two infants' classes, but with two terms to go before moving to the Junior school, had reached Beacon Infant Reader 3 and some had already started on Beacon 4. All had a thorough knowledge of letter-sounds." (*The Challenge of Reading Failure* edited by Margaret Cox and based on the N.F.E.R. Kent Survey 1968).

It is increasingly recognised that children mature at different rates and therefore that some at the age of seven are not really established in reading skill. In view of this fact it is disquieting to find in the Kent Survey that at the time of transfer to the Junior school "about 45 per cent of the children still needed the kind of teaching associated with the Infants' school"; it was also found "that approximately 75 per cent of (first year junior) teachers had no training in infant methods, 52 per cent had no experience in an Infants' school, and about 18 per cent were neither familiar with infant methods nor had any knowledge of how to teach beginning reading" (*Reading in the Primary School*). Granted the dilemmas with which teachers of infants and young juniors are faced, this chapter proposes to examine in greater detail how the teacher who believes that "play is the principal means of learning in early childhood" (*Children and their Primary Schools*, paragraph 523) and also that it is important that children should learn to read, may achieve both of these objectives. This achievement cannot be a haphazard operation.

1.   *New developments: advantages and the problems posed*

It may be helpful to examine briefly some current developments in the practice of educating young children, and to consider both how these practices affect children's desire to learn, and how systematic learning can be incorporated into them. The growing belief in schools in the value of children's learning through discovery and experience means that there is urgent need for this kind of learning situation to be well conceived and organised. Learning points must be recognised and developed by feeding in new and suitable materials and information. These beliefs have produced their effect both on school buildings and on the organisation of the timetable. There are sound educational reasons for these changes but they also present challenges.

In order to promote more learning through experience, school buildings have taken into account children's need for space and the desirability of areas being planned with certain kinds of activity in mind. Architects nowadays tend to plan so that these areas are shared by more than one class. Although this innovation may partly have been inspired by the need to keep within cost limits, it has in fact many educational advantages. Open planning is in line with the growing practice among teachers to keep their classroom doors open so that children mix with others of different ages as they play in every available space. It also reflects a growing willingness among teachers to make their skills and ideas available to children in other classes besides their own. Open planning has implications for following and encouraging children's progress in reading, for one teacher's children may spread out over an area that is larger than the normal classroom; and she must find ways of knowing about their activities and their progress in certain skills, including, of course the skill of reading.

Secondly, encouraging children to pursue their own interests in a well-prepared environment leads towards a timetable in which there are few fixed times when everything is packed away whether it is finished or not. Generally, set times are for the use of shared facilities like the hall, or for communal activities like the religious assembly. The free day gives children freedom, but places a responsibility upon the teacher for organising the different areas of work so that children can use them purposefully and in a way that develops self-reliance. The teacher is not a slave to freedom, but is ready to modify the daily programme to meet the needs of her children at a particular time. She has also to feed in resources as the need for them arises, and observe carefully the development of individual

1.   Words gain meaning from sensory experience

2. Putting reading to practical use

3. The reading corner: an essential part of the infants' classroom

4.   Reading can take place in a variety of contexts at the same time

3. The reading corner: an essential part of the infants' classroom

4. Reading can take place in a variety of contexts at the same time

children. The effective use of her own time will include listening, talking, helping to clarify children's ideas, teaching groups, and of course hearing reading.

Active learning is still in the process of being understood and developed. A possible danger is that the classroom can easily become stereotyped. The provision of basic materials like sand, clay, water, paint, wood and waste materials may become automatic so that teachers cease to think about them, add to them or present them differently. Active learning is perhaps only fully achieved when the teacher is active with her children, seeing the possibilities of materials and recognising growing points.

2. Incentives for reading and writing

Active learning, if it is wisely and sensitively employed by the teacher, provides children with strong incentives to learn to read and to write. It also encourages language development. There is a growing acceptance among teachers of the importance of fluency in spoken language, both for its own sake and as a preliminary to learning to read. This, of course, is not a new development, for the importance of children learning to express themselves in speech has long been recognised in Infants' schools, and the class news period was an early attempt to get children talking about familiar happenings, their families, their birthdays, and the things they did after school like visiting their grannies, and going out shopping. Friendly and warm relationships still encourage the exchange of news of this kind, but it most often happens informally—for example, through the child's spontaneous conversation when he arrives at school—rather than in a formally organised news period.

The change of emphasis in recent years springs from the fact that conversation is seen to be an integral part of active learning, and active learning is seen to provide a wealth of opportunities for language development. "Experience and language interact all the time; words come to life in the setting of sensory experience and vivid imaginative experience. It is equally true that experience becomes richer when talked over and recreated." (Children and their Primary Schools, paragraph 579).

From their earliest days in school children are encouraged to talk with their teachers as they play. At first they may do little more than draw the attention of their teacher to what they are doing. "Look, I've made a bridge." "Watch how fast I can run." At this early stage teachers can do much to increase the range of words that children can understand and use. They may do it by sitting down, for example, with the child who has made the bridge with bricks and leading him to talk about the kinds of bricks he has used; the long ones and short ones and how he has made them balance; the vehicles that would go over the bridge, and whether any would go under it. The possibilities for conversation are endless, and the teacher's skill lies in recognising the moment when a child is ready to talk about what he is doing. She can also introduce into the environment materials and situations that encourage speech.

In photograph 1, opposite page 8, children in their first year in school have enjoyed the sensory experience of being able to handle a collection of objects with different textures. Gathering them in a group, the teacher has talked with them about the things they have touched. She has then made a list of the words they have used in describing their experiences. Objects with distinctive smells and sounds have also been collected and discussed, and in this way experience has been enriched, and through experience children have added to the number of words they can use or understand. In this case they have also seen these words expressed as written symbols.

Opportunities for speech that is related to experience are important for all children and particularly for those whose pre-school experience has been limited by socially and culturally deprived conditions. Children need to be able to talk about first-hand experiences within the classroom and also to extend their experience beyond the classroom through visits to local shops, parks and places of interest. Experience can sometimes be enriched if the school has a collection of transparencies or casettes for use with 8 mm. loop projectors, as well as the more usual aids of pictures and books through which children can extend knowledge that has begun through situations met at first-hand.

For example, a four-minute loop of ducks nesting and swimming can follow up a visit to the local park and watching ducks there. The children can talk with their teacher about the colours of the ducks and the movements they make as they swim. Or a series of transparencies brought back by the teacher from a holiday abroad showing a street market can provide talking points after a visit to the local stall and shops. Opportunities for the first-hand experience and follow-up can be almost limitless.

One limitation however lies, not so much in the teacher's lack of ingenuity in recognising or stimulating points of interest, as in the time that is available for the different facets of her job. While she is talking and listening to children she cannot hear reading, and while she is hearing reading she cannot be helping children to build mathematical concepts. But, in fact, language in one form or another is a part of almost all the things she does with her children. It is through talking with children as they play—for instance, with sand or water—that she helps them to clarify their thinking and to build mathematical concepts. It is through listening and talking to them as they experiment with the objects on the discovery table that she helps them to observe, to think and to reason. As they select from the waste materials for their modelling she can lead them to talk about which material will best achieve a certain purpose, and so they begin to make judgements. Their ability to use language will also increase as they listen to stories and poetry, or as they talk about the sounds they make with the instruments in the music corner.

Most children want to talk about the things they do, and if the teacher recognises this desire and is sensitive to the stage that individual children have reached she can greatly extend their ability to use and to understand spoken language.

Providing opportunities for this dialogue between children and adults should be one of the main concerns of the teacher. She may be helped by other adults, and although their skill may vary, part-time teachers, students, visitors, auxiliary helpers and parents can all usefully listen and talk to individual children. Often the enthusiasm and interest of the headmistress as she moves round the school makes her very much sought after as a listener and contributor to children's thinking.

For the child to become articulate at his own level is important, and the seriously inarticulate child is not ready to read. The Plowden Report (paragraph 581) stresses the need for fluent speech: ". . . there is reason for grave concern about those children who get to the top of the Infants' school, and even more, the lower reaches of the Junior school before they have become fluent in speech. If teachers are over anxious to establish literacy at this stage they may concentrate too narrowly on graded readers and spend too little time on stories. They may clamp down on children's interests and on the conversation and planning arising from them, even though they provide an incentive for reading and writing." Clarity of speech is also important, and serious speech defects may impede progress in reading. Children suffering from handicaps of this kind probably need early and skilled help from a speech therapist.

An ability to use language that is related to experience is a prime requirement for learning to read. Alongside it must go a desire to learn to read, and this desire is kindled and fed in many ways in an active classroom. One of the main requirements is that the captions that the teacher writes for models, paintings or collections of various kinds, the notices with which she guides the children in using and maintaining the environment and the text that she writes in their news or story books should reflect their real interests and activities. If this is so they are at least likely to have an incentive to read what is written, and their need to read it will not have to be unduly contrived by the teacher. Typical of reading matter that is related to children's activities and interests are class or group books recording visits out of school, captioned block graphs and diagrams recording mathematical investigations and short accounts of individual or group interests within the classroom. These last may come and go quickly and they have tended to replace the exquisitely produced wall story. In some activities children are assisted by cards written by the teacher or by simple books that offer guidance. For example, the seven-year-olds in photograph 2, opposite page 8, are making bread and using a simple recipe that the teacher has written and which they are anxious to follow so that their bread comes out right. In the same classroom the teacher had made cards suggesting how children might experiment with pendulums, leaving them to find out and record the result.

Written expression is at first almost always a record of experience. The five-year-old may ask his teacher to write "*I made a bus with boxes. Here it is*", and he may draw a picture of the bus he has made with waste materials. Sometimes he will copy his teacher's writing, but the main point is that he sees the written words as symbols expressing what he has said. Some quite young children dictate long or unexpected sentences or descriptions for the teacher to write. Again, what matters is not so much that the child shall write over or under her writing as that he sees the written words as expressing meaning, *his* meaning. At this stage the spoken and the written word begin to be linked, and children gradually begin to write for themselves. But it is a mistake to press children to write by themselves too soon. If they are not forced, and if the kind of aids are available that are described elsewhere in this book, many children will be capable of quite lively descriptive writing. For example, a seven-year-old experimenting with magnets described clearly what he had done:

"This morning I was working with magnets and I found that if I put some pins on the floor then pick one up with a magnet, then try picking another one up the pin that you already have will pick up the other one."

Another child of nearly seven years described what happened when he spun balls in the sand:

"I did this in the sand and I was spinning some balls and some balls did not spin then I began to wonder about the marks so I chose 7 balls made of different things and different sizes and I span them again. I was surprised at what I saw.
I saw that the small light table-tennis ball made a deeper cleaner mark than the heavy golf ball.
The coloured air ball moved about and made a splodgy mark.
The big rubber ball went right through the sand and showed a round spot in the middle which was the tray underneath and I would not have expected that the big rubber ball would have made such an untidy mark.
I measured the circumference with tape and put it by the mark each ball made to show the size."

This was accurate observation clearly described.
Sometimes children express a mixture of descriptive and imaginative thought, like the child who wrote, after a music and movement lesson:

"When I was a snowflake I really felt like one. I twisted and twirled around. I imagined that all my surroundings were white I went up and down and all around and slowly but gentley I touched the ground and stayed there.
That's what I think happens to a snowflake."

Sometimes the imagination takes over more actively, as when a six-year-old wrote:

"it was a suny shining day and the black cat went out. his coat glisnd in the sun sudenly it began to rain the rain splaterd on to his glisning coat and distrouyed the streak of light across his fur he tride to run but the wind held him bake it rained till night. to big eyes perd out of a tree oh the cat jumpd. his tail frild."

If they are to write in this way children must have heard language vividly used in stories and in poetry and they must not feel fettered by the need to spell every word correctly. Spelling matters but not at the time when all the child's energies are directed towards saying what he wants to say.

The incentive to read and to write that comes from looking at books and being read to has probably increased with the spectacular improvement in recent years in the quality of books for young children. Artist-writers like Brian Wildsmith, John Burningham and Charles Keeping—to mention only three of a growing number—have produced books that have suitable texts and are brilliantly illustrated in a contemporary idiom. Publishers are also producing an encouraging number of simple and clearly illustrated books of reference. Some local authorities keep schools up to date in information about new books; some make books available on loan, and in many areas public libraries are interested in lending books to children of Infants' school age. The book corner is an essential part of the infants' classroom. Here, children can explore and enjoy books and poetry, reading quietly by themselves, sometimes reading to each other and from time to time trying to reread stories that have been read by the teacher. The book corner in photograph 3, opposite page 9, has been carefully arranged. The background theme on this occasion is one of horses; the teacher has provided a length of suitable fabric, and the children themselves have brought articles for the display. A homely atmosphere is suggested by the provision of a small piece of carpet.

In planning new schools, account is taken of the need for a central reference library. The tendency is not to shut this collection of books away behind a closed door, but to create a central library and exhibition space, making strongly the point that books are both attractive to look at and easily available for use.

In recent years primers, too, have become rather more attractive so that there is a stronger incentive to read them. In particular, pre-readers are short, well produced, covering a range of subjects, well illustrated and still relatively inexpensive. They meet very adequately the needs of children who are not yet ready for systematic work with one or a combination of several reading series. Most of the primers, however, although they have improved in general layout and illustration, do not yet fully meet the needs of all children. Even by using a combination of several series it may be difficult to find subject matter that takes into account a wide range of social and cultural backgrounds. This deficiency is regrettable, as teachers who are at full stretch in providing children with incentives to read need to be supported by good published material which helps them to acquire the complex and difficult techniques.

3. Techniques of teaching reading

There is also the problem of children who are slow to begin to read, and a teacher must look for the causes of delay and find ways of giving help that is well-timed and suited to individual needs. The fact that children who have made little or no start in reading in the Junior school or even in their last year in the Infants' school may suffer from a sense of personal failure that extends beyond their failure to read makes it imperative that we should continually re-examine the techniques and methods that we employ in helping them to acquire this skill. As has already been indicated, there are some conflicting views and account is taken of these in what follows.

(a) *Reading readiness.* There is a wide variety of practice among teachers in timing the beginning of systematic learning and teaching. The belief that children are not ready for systematic help before they reach a mental or even a chronological age of six has been widespread and may have resulted in some children being held back unnecessarily. The Hadow Report's comment, "it is well known that the postponement of formal instruction does not handicap the child in the long run", is a statement based on Professor Burt's assertion that "there should be little or no formal instruction before the age of six at the earliest" and has undoubtedly influenced teachers' thinking and practice. The argument for delaying systematic teaching can also be supported by the fact that in most other countries the age of entry to school (and therefore presumably of learning to read) is later than it is in this country and that this does not appear to affect standards of literacy in the later stages of education. Nonetheless, it has to be borne in mind that the findings of Dr Joyce Morris in the Kent Survey seem to be in direct opposition to this point of view. The Survey suggested that the schools which taught reading most successfully were those that began systematic and formal teaching in the reception class. It seems likely, however, or at least possible, that teachers who believe it necessary to give their children early, systematic instruction in reading may be less successful in providing young children with an active learning situation that encourages their ability to think, to reason and in which general language development is promoted. The Plowden Report (paragraph 28) suggests that for many children there may be periods of optimum readiness for acquiring certain skills. If this is so, premature forcing and undue delay are equally to be avoided. To suggest that precisely the right time can be found may seem to be a counsel of perfection. Probably many teachers find approximately the right time for most children. Their judgement will be based on the interest that individual children show in the captions and notices that are related to the day-to-day life of the classroom, and on their ability to associate the written or printed symbol with meaning; it will take into account children's ability to use and to understand spoken language; and it will also depend upon children's general maturity and on the way they have settled into school. Finding the right time for systematic learning and teaching is an exercise to which teachers need constantly to address their minds.

Some children from favoured and "bookish" backgrounds may be reading before they come to school, although, of course this does not necessarily follow. Some will very quickly be ready to read. But others, and in this number will be included many from Educational Priority Areas, will need opportunities for widening their experiences and (as suggested earlier in the chapter) for talking and listening and for becoming familiar with the written and printed word as a part of everyday life. In all classes the range of ability will be wide; different children will be ready to read at different times and one of the most difficult tasks that the teacher faces is that of giving the slow starter the necessary period of preparation and at the same time protecting him from discouragement. While the final summing up of the Hadow Report that "the child should begin to learn the three Rs when he wants to do so, whether he be three or six years old" is broadly true, the skill of the teacher still lies partly in determining whether the three-year-old wants to read because of pressure from a parent or older sibling, and in ensuring that the six or seven-year-old does eventually experience some desire to read. These are informed professional judgements.

(b) *Methods of teaching reading.* Most teachers in Infants' schools use a mixture of sentence, whole word and phonic methods and the differences between them lie mainly in the emphasis that they give to the various methods, and in particular to the method that predominates in the early stages of learning to read. The sentence method, placing reading in the context of interest and meaning, seems to be most in line with modern methods of educating young children. But the fact that the Kent Survey has shown that children who learnt phonics early read more successfully than those who did not, and that many slow readers in the first years in the Junior school have no knowledge of letter names and sounds and therefore are unable to make any attack upon new words, seems to indicate that teachers should look again at the place of phonic teaching in the whole process of learning to read. Children can be helped to want to learn to read and to see its relevance if, from the beginning, they meet the written or printed word in situations where it has meaning or is of practical use. For example, a notice in the classroom saying

"Please hang your aprons here"

will be used by the children every day and will have more meaning for them than labels attached to various pieces of furniture. To start with a phonic approach to reading may easily result in learning to read words and sentences that reflect neither children's interests nor their natural vocabulary. They may be motivated only by desire to please the adult and it is likely that, initially at least, reading will be a skill divorced from the rest of their interests and activities. The view of many educationists is that for young children the emphasis should be upon the wholeness of learning,

B

and that a fragmentation of the curriculum into distinct areas does not produce the most favourable learning situation.

This is not to say that there is no place for informal phonic teaching even at an early stage, and many teachers draw attention to the initial letters of words as they are writing in children's books or adding captions to pictures and models. In this way teachers are helped to identify the children for whom a slightly phonic bias may be appropriate, and the children themselves begin to be aware of letter sounds.

A few children learn to read without using primers but for most the progression will be from the simple books, sentences and words that are a part of the classroom environment, to the sight vocabulary of the graded reader. Most graded readers build up a sight vocabulary which the children are helped by the teacher to learn as they move from page to page and from book to book. The time comes, however, when new words come too quickly for this method to be practicable, and this seems to be the logical time for learning phonics. It is disquieting that those children who need it do not always get this teaching in a way that enables or at least helps them to attack new words. When the time comes (this is often at about Book 2 or Book 3 of the reading series) the teaching should be carefully given but not laboured. The scheme of work for reading (or failing this, the teacher herself) should set out what single sounds, double sounds and groups of letters are to be learnt. Not all children will need this help. Many do. Time may not allow for this teaching to be given to individual children, but it can be given to a small group that is roughly at the same stage. Phonic practice should be given in short periods (say of five minutes), and although it is often helpful to relate it to known words or words from the reading book, systematic practice is best given at a time when the children are not reading from books, so that flow and reading for meaning are not hindered by it. This precise teaching of phonics may seem to be at variance with the free day in which the children have a large measure of freedom to choose their activities. It is perfectly possible, however, for the teacher to gather a small group round her, and indeed if the teaching space is arranged in areas of work there is less problem about what the rest of the children are to do than there would be in a more formally organised class.

(c) *Practice and apparatus.* Phonic practice is only one aspect of learning to read. Time has also to be found for practice (for example with flash cards) in word recognition and in reading aloud from a book. Finding time to hear children read without giving too much time to this one aspect of learning has always been a problem. Certainly children need some practice in reading each day when they are at the stage of spurting into reading. This practice need not always be in reading from a primer and can include reading what they themselves have written, or reading that is connected with group or class activities. But when children are beginning to get a feeling of success they make it very clear that they want to read aloud from their books. It is particularly useful in this situation to have an extra adult in the classroom who can listen, talk, and be interested in what the rest of the children are doing and so free the teacher to give more time to reading than she might otherwise do.

The tendency, when teachers are encouraging children to learn actively, is for them to dispense with the apparatus and practice material that is intended to help children to consolidate certain skills. Nevertheless it is arguable that a moderate amount of practice may give confidence to children who are slow to learn. Practice of this kind should not, of course, be used merely as a time-filler, nor is it incompatible with a free timetable and an active approach to learning. Preferably it should include games that give practice in word recognition rather than exercises that require a level of handwriting and manual dexterity that is out of all proportion to their value. The aim is to provide practice that gives confidence and not drudgery that kills enthusiasm. Children's need for practice must be assessed individually, and in a classroom where areas of work are carefully organised, where materials are easily seen and where children can help themselves, practice falls into place alongside all the other possible activities.

(d) *Other aids to learning to read.* There are inevitably difficulties in learning to read a language that does not readily lend itself to consistent phonic analysis, and from time to time there have been attempts to provide a greater measure of consistency in early reading material or to provide clues (for example by the use of certain colours for certain sounds) that will help children to decode the printed word. Probably the best known of these aids to reading is the Initial Teaching Alphabet whose forty-six symbols invariably represent the same spoken sounds. There are both advantages and disadvantages in using this medium. The obvious advantage of its consistency which enables children to be self-reliant in reading unfamiliar words has to be weighed against the difficulties that the less able children may experience in transferring to traditional orthography and against the fact that unless the medium is very widely used there will inevitably be limitations upon the range and number of books that are available. The value of an aid of this kind cannot be accurately assessed until it has been tried over a long enough period for the Hawthorne effect (that is the effect of the teachers' heightened enthusiasm for a new venture which in its turn affects the children) has had time to stabilise. Present indications are that the early claims that were made for the efficacy of I.T.A. as a medium for learning to read may not be sustained in the longer term, and in particular for the least able children who can experience considerable difficulty in transferring to traditional orthography. It may find its place as a medium which some teachers find to be effective in a particular situation. The same is probably true of Reading in Colour. Although there is not an orthographic problem here, children must eventually learn to do without the help of colour.

(e)   *Meeting the needs of the individual children.* Dr Goodacre in her book *Reading in Infant Classes* reports finding that teachers are slow to adjust their methods to children with special needs or to neighbourhoods whose characteristics seem to indicate that a difference in the timing of teaching reading or a difference in the content of the reading material would be helpful. For example, some children are given a primer long before they are mature, experienced or fluent enough in speech to be ready for it; some children who are slow to begin reading are relentlessly presented with whole sentences when a whole-word method or a more phonic bias might suit them better. And in Educational Priority Areas the graded readers tell of middle class children doing and saying unfamiliar things in what, for the children who read them, are almost totally strange surroundings. There is a challenge in these assertions that some publishers are beginning to meet by producing books in the idiom of particular groups of children. More still needs to be done. Teachers themselves cannot escape this challenge, as it seems certain that some children would be more successful in learning to read if timing, method and the actual reading material were related more closely to their needs and their interests.

4. *The need for continuity*

A scheme of work which takes into account children's interests and how they may be used, the varying rates at which they learn to read and the methods best suited to differing needs, can be a valuable working guide for teachers. In some Infants' schools discussions between head teachers and their staffs ensure that there is a measure of agreement about the methods and materials that are used, but even where there is collaboration of this kind, some written guidance is helpful for inexperienced teachers or for those who are only in the school for a short time. Children are needlessly confused if, as they move from one class to another (and this often happens in the course of the year as well as at the end of it) there is a sharp break in the methods used or in the attitude and expectation of the teachers. Continuity is important, and if children must change classes it is essential that the new teacher should receive detailed information about the child's progress so far. Passing on this information should be easy within an Infants' school. However, this does not always happen and continuity is needlessly broken.

The need for continuity as children move from the Infants' to the Junior school is particularly urgent, as this move takes place at the end of a long holiday during which much that may have been rather precariously known has now been forgotten. The move also involves getting used to a new building and different teachers, and the adjustment to being the youngest children in the new school rather than the oldest ones in the school that has just been left. The facts about lack of continuity in learning to read revealed by the N.F.E.R. Kent Survey have been referred to earlier in this chapter. It seems essential that many more junior teachers should know how to teach beginning reading, and in the long term this is a matter for the initial and in-service training of teachers. In the shorter term however, there is much that can be done to improve matters both by infants' teachers and by the junior teachers in the schools to which their children transfer.

Teaching reading is the joint task of Infants' and Junior schools, and not only Primary-school teachers but those who teach general subjects to the less able children in the lower forms of Secondary schools should understand their difficulties and be able to help them. In Primary schools that contain the full age range of five to eleven plus, advantage can be taken of the fact that children do not change schools at seven plus, that their teachers are members of a single staff and that it is relatively easy for them to share their expertise and to exchange information about children's progress. Even in this favourable situation continuity is not inevitably achieved and the advantages of a full-range Primary school are not always fully exploited. In a Junior mixed and Infants' school it should be easy to think not of 'infants' and 'juniors' but of children whose development, including the acquisition of language skills, is the concern of the whole staff.

The advantages and disadvantages of separate and combined schools need not be examined here, but where schools are separate it is certain that detailed attention must be given to achieving continuity at the point of transfer. In many pairs of schools there is a general attitude of goodwill rather than careful attention to the methods and materials that are used by each school. In schools where the importance of continuity is accepted, teachers find many ways of trying to secure it. In the summer term, junior teachers who are to be responsible for first year classes in September spend some time with the seven-year-olds, getting to know them and seeing how far they have progressed—for example, in learning to read—and becoming familiar with the methods that are used. In some cases they work alongside the infants' teachers observing the children at first hand so that the written records that are passed on at the end of the term serve only to summarise and add precision to their own knowledge. Less frequently, infants' teachers visit junior classes, watching the development of children, and setting their own work into the pattern of children's ways of learning throughout the whole primary stage. Teachers need to be convinced of the value of this kind of collaboration if they are to find time for it amid the many commitments of the summer term. Obviously visits can take place at other times, but in the summer term it is possible to see the standards children have reached before the blurring effect of the long summer holiday. Passing on folders with samples of children's work, and the books they are currently reading also helps the receiving teacher to form a clear idea of each child's stage of development in the different areas of the curriculum.

Some pairs of schools arrange joint staff meetings at which different aspects of the curriculum are discussed. One or other of the head teachers or a teacher with a particular interest or skill may start the discussion off by giving a short talk. The teaching of reading is an obvious subject for a discussion of this kind.

In other schools the head teachers, helped sometimes by members of their staffs, co-operate in making schemes of work that flow smoothly on from the five-year-old to the eleven-year-old stage. Continuity becomes an attainable objective if these schemes are given to all members of both staffs.

Different schools will devise ways that are appropriate to their own situation of avoiding sharp breaks in learning. Many are increasingly realising the importance of making opportunities for parents to get to know the new school and its teachers so that they can share with their children what can be the exciting experience of moving into the "big school".

5. *The role of parents*

If parents know about and understand the methods the school is using to educate their children, the children themselves are more likely to be successful. This, for many teachers, is an obvious fact. Their belief that parents who are interested in what their children do at school often have children who like school and do well is supported by the National Survey of Parental Attitudes, undertaken at the request of the Plowden Council, which showed that parental attitude influences children's attainment more than social class or the state of the school they attend. What is not clear is how parental attitudes may be influenced; but an exercise in a London school (described in a book by Dr Michael Young and Patrick McGeeney and called *Learning Begins at Home* [Routledge & Kegan Paul, 1968]) suggests that if their attitudes are to affect children's attainment favourably, parents must have detailed knowledge and experience of the kinds of things their children learn at school.

Practice in Primary schools is moving towards giving parents more information, welcoming them into school and involving them in many of its activities. Meetings of the parents of new entrants aim at explaining modern methods of education. In particular, parents often need re-assuring about methods which differ from those by which *they* learnt. Parents, as they bring their children into school, build up their impression of the ways in which their children learn. Class open days, when the head teacher or part-time teachers enable the class teacher to be free to discuss children's work with their parents, help to give the necessary detailed knowledge. Parent teacher associations, parents' meetings and their involvement in aspects of the life of the school all help towards a closer understanding. It is becoming a commonplace for parents to be among the adults who take children out on visits; parents' rooms are being incorporated into the plans of some new schools; and in the process of helping children to read, some parents stay for a short while at the beginning of the day, sitting with their own child and perhaps a group of his friends and listening to them read. This contribution can be a valuable one, as it gives children the satisfaction of reading aloud to an adult. It also gives parents the satisfaction of contributing to the life of the school.

Perhaps "satisfaction" is a key word in describing our objectives as we help children to read. We try to time their learning so that they have the satisfaction of being successful from the beginning, to relate reading to activity and interest so that children experience satisfaction in using the skill they are achieving, and to adjust the pace of learning so that even children who are slow to start meet reading in situations where the pleasures of success are possible.

Chapter 1

LEARNING TO READ: SOME UNDERLYING PRINCIPLES

THE modern Infants' school has evolved through the experiments, theories and enthusiasm of educationists over a long period of years. Smaller classes, better school buildings and equipment, and an ever-increasing understanding of how children learn, have been factors that have helped to make the development of modern methods possible. These methods have been practised and their results tested. Both the teachers who have tried the methods, and the investigators who have scientifically evaluated their work, are agreed about the value and success of the modern approach.

The purpose of this book therefore, is not to defend the methods of the modern Infants' school, for these have been tried and need no defence. The aim is to state clearly the facts upon which our methods are based, and then in the light of these facts to discuss a technique of teaching reading that has proved in experience to be both practicable and successful.

A clear statement on the application of modern methods to the teaching of reading would, no doubt, serve a useful purpose. Among experienced teachers who are still using the earlier methods there are those who, while in general agreement with the modern approach, would welcome some guidance in its practical application. Among young teachers entering the profession and finding themselves for the first time responsible for teaching children to read, many may feel that they need some detailed help. There may also be many parents who would appreciate the opportunity to learn about methods that were not in use when they were at school.

It is with these three classes of people in mind that our methods of teaching reading will be examined and discussed. The main experience of the writer was gained in a post-war London Infants' school. Talking to groups of teachers in other parts of the country, however, and discussing with them both their successes and their difficulties, has led to the conviction that these methods can rightly and successfully be used wherever children are learning to read.

We need to have two aims when we teach children to read. First, we should try to discover the best way of teaching the individual child *how* to read. At the same time, we should not be so taken up with technique and method that we forget our second aim, which is to guide the child in his choice of *what* to read. If we give our children only the tool of reading, they may, as adults, progress no farther than to read those daily newspapers that demand the least thought. If, in addition, we try to pass on to them a love of books, their later reading may be of the kind that will give them real and lasting pleasure. Both method and material are important.

The tasks of teaching the child both how to read and what to read fall increasingly to the lot of the school. With the coming of wireless, television and the cinema there are many homes where books have no place. Looking and listening take much of the time of parents and children alike, so that there is little time or quiet for reading or being read to. This is especially true of children who are too young to be inspired to read and investigate for themselves as a result of what they see or hear on television or wireless. In homes where both parents go out to work, there is often even less leisure and opportunity for reading. It is unlikely that in such homes children will come to love and value books as a part of the daily environment. We must review our ideas in the light of these changed circumstances; we need to be sure that the reasons for our methods are sound; and we should also take time occasionally to ask ourselves if we are giving our children the widest and fullest approach to reading that is possible in our circumstances.

To teach a child to read, as all practising teachers know, is an exacting task, demanding skill, patience and ingenuity. It is a worth while task, but one that is not complete if we have not also awakened in him a love of books and of reading. Such an attitude to reading will arise partly from the satisfaction and sense of achievement that come as the skill is successfully mastered. It is also something that our children will, as it were, "catch" from us. It is our whole attitude that the children will imitate and to which they will respond.

If enthusiasm for reading arises in some measure from the sense of achievement, our methods must be such that right from the beginning the child has a feeling not of frustration and failure, but of achievement and success. An older child can see a distasteful task as a means of achieving a remote, but desirable, goal. For the younger child, however, the task needs to be of immediate interest. If he is successful in the early stages his success will be an incentive to further effort. This sense of achievement and success will be most likely to arise if we can base our methods of teaching upon known facts about how the child naturally learns and develops.

Psychology has done much to help us here. Experiments carried out both in Europe and in America have established certain facts about the way in which young children learn. Among the more important of these facts are:

(*a*) Young children learn most readily when their interest is aroused.
(*b*) Children recognize sentences, phrases and words by their general pattern or shape before they have been taught letters or sounds.
(*c*) Children develop mentally at different rates.

1. *The importance of interest as a factor in learning to read*

To say that it matters that the child should be interested in learning to read may appear at first to be obvious. When, however, we consider the dreary nature of much of the first reading material that children meet, we realize that the importance of interest as a factor affecting learning still needs to be stressed. It is true that we have progressed beyond such depressing examples as, "*Nod to Ned Nan. Can Nan nod to Ned?*" or, "*Put the stale cake on the plate and give it to the pale old man.*" But some of the material that children meet, especially in the early stages of learning to read, is not of the kind that will arouse their interest and stimulate in them a desire to read more.

We may understand the children better if we consider our own experience as adults when we try to learn something new. The situations are not exactly parallel, as in our case there are factors affecting our learning that do not obtain with children. We can use our wills to help us to concentrate in achieving a distant and worth-while end. We may have to learn in order to pass an examination, or we may decide to acquire some knowledge that will help us to do our daily job more efficiently. In neither case need there be an overwhelming interest in the actual subject that is learned.

We know from experience how much more easily we learn when our interest is aroused. With very little effort of will we can apply ourselves for long stretches of time to our hobbies. It is this spontaneous application to a task that is interesting that we try to use in teaching young children to read. In the beginning, children will apply themselves for the most part to things they like doing, but by the time they go to the Junior school many of them will begin to be capable of the concentration that is the result of conscious effort.

The under-fives in our nursery class are free to choose from a wide variety of activities. Although the attention of very young children tends to pass quickly from one occupation to the next, here and there a child's interest will be held for a considerable period. When this happens, he often progresses towards the perfecting of the skills required in the particular activity in which he is engaged, and in doing so he gets a feeling of success which makes him want to do it all over again.

For instance, Robert, aged four, sat doing a jigsaw puzzle over and over again. The picture was of a bus "like my Daddy drives", so that Robert's interest was captured. He also experienced a sense of achievement from doing the puzzle correctly every time. Peter, also aged four, polished the door-handles of the nursery every day for days on end. He was interested because it was something he had seen his mother do, and he experienced great satisfaction in imitating her. It was satisfying, too, to receive the approval of the grown-ups who happened to pass along the corridor while he was at work.

Although a young child will apply himself for a considerable period to a task in which he is really interested, his goal needs to be an immediate one. Robert's puzzle was not of the kind that takes hours to complete, and Peter could quite soon make his door-handles shining and bright. Both experienced quickly the feeling of achievement which is a spur to further effort. Most children in the nursery will not be mentally ready to begin to acquire the skills of reading, writing and number, although very occasionally we find a child who is ready to begin to read at this early age. By watching the play of these young children, we can learn much about their natural interests, and it is upon these interests that their first reading material will be based.

Interest grows and widens with the mental development of the child. Richard, aged six, was a heavy, slow child who did not seem attracted by anything, until one day his imagination was fired by the collection of "junk" material that was part of the classroom equipment. He used this material for many days, and during this time he established himself as leader of a group of boys who made a large model of a pleasure steamer. Richard developed noticeably with the sense of power that came from this leadership.

Reading material was based on the making of the model, and Richard began to be interested in drawing and writing about what he was doing. This and the sense of achievement that came from his success in making the steamer, helped Richard through the first steps of learning to read. In this case the interest was sustained for a longer period than with the nursery children. Richard's reading material arose spontaneously from a current activity. His first reading book was home-made and personal to him, not a primer containing material unrelated to things he liked. He was still at the stage of needing interest to help him to concentrate and learn.

Older children are capable of harnessing their will to their interest, or of using it to help them to complete a task, needing to be done but not immediately attractive. Andrea, aged twelve, spent the whole of a wet afternoon with her stamp collection. An accumulation of stamps needed sorting and mounting, and she carried on this task patiently and persistently in the face of many distractions. There were other much more interesting occupations possible, but this was not a passing whim. It was a hobby requiring an effort of will and the ability to visualize a distant goal—in this case the building up of an extensive and well-ordered stamp collection. Such is the concentration of the older child, beginning in some cases with interest, but capable of being sustained when this is on the wane, so that a task may be satisfactorily completed.

An outstanding characteristic of the child when he enters the Infants' school is the attraction his immediate environment holds for him. He is interested both in the things that happen to him and in those that take place around him. He is eager to talk about the things he does with his mother and father, and to tell us about his baby, his birthday party, or his new clothes. He is delighted with his increasing manipulative skill, and anxious for our approval of his painting, or the tall tower he has made with his bricks.

When he first comes into school, the child should have the opportunity to talk freely about all these things that engage his attention, for the ability to use words in speech must come before learning to read and write them. Our task is to observe the child's natural interests and to give him freedom to talk to us, and to other children about them, since they give rise directly to the early work in reading, writing and number.

In approaching reading through interest the natural sequence is: first, that the child has something he wants to say, second, that we write it down for him, and last, that he reads it, and *wants* to read it because it tells of something that is of real interest to him.

In the reception class three boys joined in making a rough and ready train from 'junk' materials. They were greatly excited about what they were doing, and when the teacher made some wall sheets about it saying:

> *"John made an engine*
> *"Terry helped him*
> *"They used boxes*
> *"They used tins"*

they greeted everyone who came into the room with the words, "We've made an engine *and* we can read about it". Such an approach to reading is more likely to meet with success than the method of presenting a sentence of "the cat sat on the mat" variety.

Interest can be a driving power, and we try to get the child's absorption in what he sees and does to overflow into reading and writing about those things. In this way the driving force of his interest will help him through the first steps of reading. To help him to acquire the skill of reading is the first of our aims. If his first reading material is alive and interesting, so that he is successful with it, there will be an association in his mind between reading and pleasure. By providing material of this sort we shall be more likely to achieve the second of our aims, and our children will grow towards a lasting and increasing delight in reading.

2. *The recognition of the shape or pattern of the sentence, phrase, or word*

Research with large numbers of children has shown that the best way to begin to teach most children to read is to present them with a whole sentence that has interest and meaning.

How will such a sentence be recognized? It will be recognized:

(*a*) Because the child has an incentive to remember the sentence. It is about something that concerns him, and it says something that he himself wanted to say.

(*b*) Because there may be a picture either drawn by the child or provided by the teacher. This will help him at first to distinguish between one sentence and another.

(*c*) Because of the length and shape, in the first place, of the sentence, and then of the phrases and words within the sentence.

A child soon after he comes to school may ask his teacher to write in his newsbook,

"John has a new aeroplane"

He will draw a picture of himself with his aeroplane and he may write with a coloured crayon over what has been written. When he next turns to that page he may be able to repeat the sentence. He will be able to do this:

(*a*) Because getting his new aeroplane was an important event and his interest remains.

(*b*) Because he will recognize the picture that he draws.

(*c*) Because he will begin to remember the shape of the whole sentence. It has quite a different shape from the one on the next page which says,

"Yesterday Mary came to tea
with me"

This second sentence begins with a long word and extends into a second line. If one watches a class of children who are beginning to learn to read, one cannot doubt their ability to remember sentences in this way.

We should be slow to use the word "reading" at this stage. At first the child repeats the phrase or sentence from memory and he recognizes it in conjunction with a picture or some other aid. The child thinks he is reading. He should be allowed to think that he is reading. He is interested, and he feels successful. Slowly, this repetition develops into real reading, and we may truly say that a child can read a word when he can recognize it in another context.

After recognizing the whole sentence, the next step is to recognize the phrases and words within the sentence. In this, too, the child is helped by meaning. The words that hold the most meaning for him are the ones that he will readily remember. Other aids to remembering are the shape or pattern of the word and its position in the sentence. In our example about John and his aeroplane, John will remember the word "*John*":

(*a*) Because it is his own name and therefore significant for him.

(*b*) Because of its position at the beginning of the sentence.

(*c*) Because of its shape, which is quite unlike the other words in the sentence.

In the same way, he will remember the word "aeroplane":

(*a*) Because it is the name of the object he was so delighted to have given him.

(*b*) Because it is the last word of the sentence.

(*c*) Because its shape is unlike that of any other word in the sentence.

"*John*" and "*aeroplane*", then, will be the two words the child will most easily remember in this sentence. His memory will be aided by the kinaesthetic experience of writing them and by matching them against duplicate words. We do not say that the child can really read the words until he can recognize them away from their original context. He may be able to match a card with the word "*John*" on it with the word "*John*" as it appears in the sentence, but when he recognizes the word in a new sentence then he is really reading it.

Two aspects of the shape of the word help the child to remember it:

(*a*) Its length.

(*b*) The relative positions of the "tall" and "tailed" letters. Thus "*aeroplane*" and "*bus*" are of easily distinguishable lengths, and "*John*" and "*Mary*" though of similar length may be distinguished one from the other by their differing distribution of "tall" and "tailed" letters.

The child's attention should not be drawn to these tall and long letters in any systematic way. Nevertheless, shape is a factor that helps him to remember a word he has met before.

Those who have not successfully used this method may argue that, if

5. Play in the nursery room prepares the child for reading by widening his
experience and increasing his vocabulary

6. Reading arising from play with bricks

words of a distinctive pattern are recognized most easily, it would surely be better to introduce these words by themselves, rather than in sentences which must include others not so easily recognizable. But the young child is deeply interested in things that happen to him and around him, and the attraction of the first sentences he meets lies in the fact that they describe exciting things that have taken place. For most children a word by itself cannot have the same significance, although there are some backward children who seem to be helped by the word-whole approach. To present the whole sentence is to link the written word from the beginning with interest and meaning in a fuller way than is possible by using one word only. Thus the sentence:

"My new dress is pink"

expresses a fact that is "news" for the child, and has more meaning and interest than the single word "*dress.*"

Some teachers hold that by presenting the whole sentence to the child right from the beginning we are giving him something that is too difficult to grasp. To them this method seems unsystematic and difficult to follow, whereas the phonic approach seems orderly, logical and safe. To those who want such a systematic method of teaching reading, we may say that neither the children we teach nor the language we seek to teach them to read can truly be called systematic. Of the first few hundred words that the child chiefly uses, very many are ones that defy logical treatment. This does not mean that our method need be haphazard and unplanned. It does mean that we try to base our reading material upon the child's natural speaking vocabulary.

There are teachers who sincerely feel that they can teach children more successfully by using phonics as the starting point than they could by using the methods described above. Of course it *is* possible for a good teacher, who has a right relationship with her children, to teach them to read by any method. Most teachers at one time or another quite rightly use a mixture of all methods. The point at issue here is not what methods we can rightly and successfully use during the process of teaching a child to read, but rather how we should *begin* to teach him so as to enlist his full co-operation. This must be decided in the light of our knowledge of how the child learns and develops.

c

The approach to reading with sentences of "The fat cat sat on the mat" variety can, in the hands of a skilful teacher, give the child the mechanics of reading. It does not follow that this is the best method of approach. The meaning of a sentence composed of words that can be phonically sounded, such as the one given above, will not help the child to have an attitude of lively interest towards reading, nor does it make use of his known ability to remember the shape of words and sentences.

Few would condemn the use of phonics in the teaching of reading. For some children they have a definite and valuable place as a tool to be used in reading new words. The question of when the child should be given this tool is one that must be considered later. But his known ability to recognize and remember sentences and words by their visual pattern is a factor that must be accepted and given full weight in our teaching of reading.

3.   Mental age as a factor in learning to read

In 1904 Binet, the distinguished French psychologist, was asked by the French Committee of Public Instruction to serve on a committee formed to deal with the problem of backward children. So that they could discriminate between laziness and lack of ability, Binet and his colleague, Simon, devised a series of graded tests which set out to measure the "mental age" of any child. This was done by fixing the norm for a certain chronological age, and then measuring the performance of any child against what was normal for his chronological age. Thus a child's "mental age" could be fixed at so many points above or below his age in years.

Since its introduction by Binet and Simon the intelligence test has been developed and improved. Many psychologists now think that no one test can give an accurate assessment of intelligence. For accurate testing a battery of tests is used, each one designed to assess a different factor. For the purpose of teaching reading the significant fact is that mental age is not synonymous with chronological age. This means that in a class of five-year-olds the mental age of the children may vary from as low as three years to as high as seven years. This fact will materially affect our teaching of reading.

Dr. Schonell, as a result of his researches, asserted that children are not mentally ready to read with a graded reading book (that is, the first book of a series) until they reach a mental age of six. It is neither practicable nor desirable for teachers to give mental tests for discovering when a child is ready to start reading. It is a lengthy process and requires special training. In any case the preparatory period provides an opportunity for the teacher to observe each child and to decide when he is ready to read in a formal and systematic way.

In whatever way we may decide to assess our children, all of us will have found from experience that in any unstreamed class there is this wide range of mental ability. This is shown very clearly in a class at the end of its first year in the Infants' school. At one extreme there will be a small group of natural readers who have read three or four books in their graded series; at the other, the slow starters who show little interest or ability in reading and who have not yet begun to read from books. Between these two extremes the children will be grouped at different levels of ability.

In our teaching it is mental age that we must consider, but we may be tempted to "push" a child before he is mentally ready. Such premature forcing will be not only unsuccessful but definitely harmful. In attempting to read before he is mentally ready, the child will experience the frustration and sense of failure that are typical of the backward reader in the Junior school. Frustration can be experienced, too, by the child who is ready to read but is held back from doing so.

In every class in the Infants' school we shall need to cater for a wide range of ability. In a class of five-year-olds there will be a few children who are ready to go ahead very quickly with learning to read. In a class of seven-year-olds there may be some children who still need the sort of work we provide in the preparatory period. Modern methods make it possible to provide for all the different mental ages in a class, by varying the reading material we put on our walls, and the books we place upon our book tables. In teaching reading in the present-day classroom, the teacher thinks in terms of the individual and the group, rather than of the class as a whole.

As he learns to read, the young child's efforts should be rewarded by the sense of achievement that comes with success. The backward reader of the Junior school is so often the child who, for a variety of reasons, has failed and lost heart and lost interest. With such a child, any method that can inspire in him new hope and new interest will have some chance of success. We are most likely to be successful in teaching reading if we study the child, as we have tried very briefly to do in this chapter, and if we base our methods on known facts about how he learns and develops. To watch his natural interests, to give him reading material based on those interests, and to present such material in a form that the individual child is able to grasp is to lead him to approach reading in a way that will be most likely to meet with the success that is so necessary to him.

PART I

THE PREPARATORY PERIOD

MANY teachers have found that the child can approach reading successfully through the work of a preparatory or pre-reading period. This period is one in which the child begins to read through interest at his own rate, not by working systematically through a series of graded reading books. Reading a series of books comes at a later stage in the child's development.

The preparatory period is necessary for a number of reasons. By playing with a wide variety of materials during the preparatory period, the child widens his experience and so adds to his vocabulary, which is a necessary preparation for learning to read. He learns to speak clearly so that his reading is not hampered by slovenly or defective speech. The approach to the difficult technique of reading is made through his natural interests so that he will be successful and confident in the early stages. And lastly, during his first months in school, the teacher is able to watch him, to assess him, and to give him the opportunity to progress at a rate that is right for his stage of development and level of ability.

Chapter 2

THE CLASSROOM ENVIRONMENT

THE need for the widening of experience that the preparatory period provides will vary according to the home background of the individual child. Some of our children who come from privileged homes will, by the time they come to school, have had many experiences such as we perhaps can remember from our own childhood. Such a child will have played with water; made mudpies in his garden or sandcastles on the beach; experimented with plastic materials, such as plasticine or pastry or dough; made his first attempt at writing and drawing; cut out things, and stuck things, and built things with his bricks. Books will have been part of his environment and he will have been read to. Most important of all, he will have been able to talk freely to his mother or his father, or some other sympathetic adult, about his play.

It is this talking about what he is doing that is so necessary as a preparation for learning to read. The child will not be successful in learning to read words that describe things that are outside his experience. For this reason we seek to extend and supplement the experience of the child from the less fortunate home. We leave him free to experiment in a carefully prepared and planned environment, and we let him talk to us and to the children round him about what he is doing. In this way the number of words that he can use with understanding will be increased. He will also become more skilled in expressing his thoughts and ideas in words.

All young children need the opportunity to experiment, to create, and to play with other children; such play is essential if their personalities are to grow and mature. Those for whom it is a new experience are the ones for whom such playing and talking is an essential part of the preparation for learning to read.

Before we plan our classroom environment we need to think carefully of the activities that a five-year-old naturally enjoys, and to consider how far his home environment has given him opportunities for them. We have to decide how we can add to and widen the experience of the child from the unprivileged home, while at the same time developing those of the child whose home life has been rich in experiences of the right sort. Some of the activities that can be used in this way are described below.

1. *Play with water*

Playing with water is an occupation which most young children enjoy, and there are few who do not find the opportunity for doing so, either with or without the approval of an adult. Even the child from the home where Mother has no time to approve such play or to organize it will play in puddles, in gutters, or in the pond in the park. For some children there will be all the joy of playing in the bath, or helping Mother on washing day, of blowing bubbles and perhaps even having a pond in their own garden. Through these varied activities they will satisfy their need to play with water, and they will begin to learn about its properties from first-hand experience.

When he comes to school at the age of five, the child will find that he is free to play with water if he wishes. There will be a zinc tray or bath full of clean water, and close by it a collection of exciting water toys. There will be boats and corks and rubber toys that float, and heavy articles that sink. There will be small containers and large ones so that he can pour water from one to the other. There will be tins with holes pierced in the bottom so that the water comes through in a spray.

At first he will play freely with the water, experimenting with it, and will be expected to conform only to those rules that are part of his training in consideration for others. The play need not be confined to the water-trolley. It may be possible occasionally to have a doll's washing day, or the Wendy House may need to be spring-cleaned. From play of this sort, the child will get all the joy that he experiences in imitating an adult, as well as the pleasure of playing with water.

The teacher will talk to small groups of children as they play. Gradually such words as "sink", "float", "heavy", "light", "spray", "full", and "empty" will be added to those that they can use with real understanding.

2. *Play with sand*

One has only to watch young children at play on a sandy beach to realize how deep is their satisfaction in what they are doing. They will be engrossed for long stretches of time in their play. They will make sandcastles with spades or with their hands, patting them into shape, tunnelling out passages, and decorating them with shapes turned out of buckets or shells. Sometimes older members of the family will be drawn into the game, and when this happens there will often be a discussion about what is going on. In this way the younger children will learn a whole group of new words.

Some of the children who come into our schools will have been fortunate enough to have had such experiences in the secure and happy atmosphere of a family holiday. Some may have had the joy of playing in a sandpit in their own garden. For many it is unfortunately true that school provides the first opportunity for play of this kind.

In the classroom, the sand can best be used in a fairly deep zinc tray, and it should be kept damp if the children are to enjoy building and modelling with it. Dry sand may also be used, for the experiences that it provides are the different ones of pouring and sifting rather than of modelling and moulding.

Near the sand tray or trolley should be kept a tray or box of sand toys. Here, there should be small spades or other implements for digging, and a selection of moulds or shapes for making pies or turrets or sand-castles. A variety of everyday objects can be used for this purpose, such as jelly moulds or plastic eggcups and containers of all sorts. From time to time, new and interesting toys can be added. In one of our classes there was on the tray of sand toys a collection of gaily-coloured paper flags stored in a jar. The children were delighted with these and used them a great deal in their play.

When they first come into school the children will play quite freely and imaginatively with sand. Sand play is always a popular activity with young children, but equally important from the point of view of the teaching of reading is the fact that they will be talking to each other, and to us, while they are playing, thus helping to build up their vocabulary. They will learn such new words as "dig", "pour", "castle", "shape", "tunnel", "sieve", "mould" and so on.

3. *Play with clay and other malleable materials*

Children enjoy playing with materials that are soft and pliable, and that can easily be moulded into different shapes. The school provides a variety of materials of this sort of which clay is probably the most satisfactory. It is a medium that is delightful to use and most children will enjoy modelling with it. From time to time the child will also have the chance of using flour and salt paste, papier-mâché, plasticine and dough.

Play with materials of this kind gives him the joy of making something; it widens his experience; and it provides an outlet for his imagination. As in all the other activities of the preparatory period, the child will talk as he plays, and so he will become increasingly ready to learn to read.

4. *Creating with junk materials*

As a preparation for learning to read, the function of play with junk materials is similar to that of the other creative activities, in that vocabulary is enriched both by the addition of words that describe the actual processes and by the child's attempts to tell us about what he has made.

Part of our classroom equipment will be a large box painted or decorated attractively, and in it will be a collection of suitable and interesting waste materials. Cardboard containers of all kinds, wheels from old toys, cotton reels, things that will make chimneys, coloured paper, silver paper, odd bits of material, tape, string and corrugated paper are all materials that the children can adapt to their own purposes. In addition to these they will need paint and brushes, satisfactory adhesives, and scissors. Interest in the junk box may fluctuate, but in most classrooms there are times when the children are vitally stimulated and challenged as they play with it.

5. *Building with bricks*

Many children older than those in the entrants' classes enjoy playing with bricks. Such play seems to have a very wide appeal. It provides an opportunity for imaginative play, and many so-called difficult children will be completely engrossed in it.

We should provide as many kinds and shapes of bricks as possible, and it is often a good idea to have a box of small toys for use with them. There can be cars, animals and small figures, and many children will enjoy incorporating these in their imaginative play.

Part of the joy in playing with bricks for the youngest children may be in knocking down again the models they have made. But many children's play will be really imaginative. It is interesting to watch them using the models they have made. They will unload ships in the dock; drive cars into the garage; make boats and then sail them under the bridge, and so on. It is helpful if the children can play where there is as much floor space as possible. If a hall is available this is a most suitable place, as here the children can spread their models over a wide area without being in anybody's way, and without the danger of having their bricks knocked over.

6. *Painting*

Painting is often one of the child's first attempts to express himself on paper. Before he comes to school he may scribble on a piece of paper with a crayon, with a pencil or with a paint brush, and tell us that "That is a spider." In the early stages we should accept what the child does. We should not attempt to criticize or show him what to do. When he first comes to school, we should try to give him the sort of atmosphere in which he is free to paint what he likes, and not what he thinks will please us. If the atmosphere in our classroom is right, then the child's first paintings will be vivid and alive.

We should give the young child a wide variety of materials and because his manipulative skill is not yet fully developed, all the materials should be large. We should give him large sheets of kitchen paper, of sugar paper and even of newspaper, and we should try to avoid it always being of the same shape. We should give him large brushes, and powder colour, both wet powder colour mixed in jars, and dry powder colour in patty tins, with a plate or saucer on which to mix the colours.

In the beginning the child will paint straight away with a brush. We should try to provide conditions where there is plenty of room for arm movement. When they have finished painting, or indeed while they are actually painting, children will often want to talk about what they have painted. Our role is to listen and to appreciate. It is never to compare or to criticize.

As well as giving our children experience in painting, we try also to let them use non-smearing crayons, chalk with large boards, and occasionally charcoal. There seems to be for them a great joy in making strong black marks. Painting is one of the child's first methods of expression. By painting he begins to externalize his thoughts. It is the forerunner of creative writing and, being another way of expressing thoughts and ideas on paper, it is closely allied to reading.

7. *Domestic play*

Most children seem to enjoy playing at mothers and fathers. Even children with little opportunity for play of this sort at home can play in this way in streets, squares, playgrounds and parks. In school we can give them such materials that they will get real joy from their play.

Children like the feeling of being able to go inside somewhere. So in our classroom we can provide either a Wendy house or a home corner made from a clothes horse covered with material or paper.

The Home Corner should be furnished with a table, chairs, a dresser, a cooker, a doll's bed and bed clothes, a pram, one or more dolls that can be dressed and undressed, a tea service and a cooking set. The dressing-up box may well be used in connection with play of this sort. The children as they play in the home corner will identify themselves with their parents or other adults. They will play out the sort of things they see happening at home.

Domestic play can be a valuable preparation for learning to read. If the early reading books tell, as it is so suitable that they should, of the everyday life of children in a family, then home play will be giving the children the same kind of experiences that they will read about there. Through these experiences the children will be adding to their vocabularies the words that they will meet in their reading books. Experience, speech, and reading will be centred upon the same theme.

8. *Learning about living and growing things*

Most young children are naturally interested in things that are alive and in things that grow. If their home is of the sort in which there is enough time and understanding to give them the right kind of experiences, by the time they come to school they will already have had the opportunity of watching and caring for living and growing things. Perhaps they will have had a pet that they have helped to look after. Almost certainly they will have helped in the garden, and they may have had their own patch of garden where they could plant seeds and watch them grow.

It is this kind of experience that we try to give our children when they come to school. The nature table is accepted as part of the environment that we provide. Those of us who teach in town schools find that it may tend to become rather a dusty and dreary affair.

If it is covered with plain-coloured American cloth, it is easy to keep the Nature Table fresh and to deal with spilt water. Ours is a town school in the midst of large blocks of flats. Few of our children have gardens of their own, and for some of them the school provides almost their only experience of growing plants. Therefore the nature table should have on it, not only the familiar little jars of neatly labelled flowers, but also things that the children really can watch as they grow. In this way we shall be achieving through interest in nature what we set out to do in the preparatory period. We shall be widening and extending the children's experiences.

It is not always a simple matter to keep pets in school. In our school, where many of the children have little opportunity for keeping pets at home, we have found that their obvious delight in having an animal in the classroom has made the venture well worth while. The children themselves feed the animals and keep them clean. They form the habit of doing this regularly and thoroughly, and they learn to be gentle with creatures that are weaker than themselves.

9. *Looking at books*

The children we teach will vary very much in the extent to which they are familiar with books. Part of our task in preparing the children to learn to read is to introduce them to books as things to be valued, and from which come pleasurable experiences.

In order to do this, we provide a book corner or book table as an essential part of the classroom environment. This is an attractively set-up and carefully kept table on which are a collection of suitable books. The teacher sits at the table and reads to a small group of children, just as mother or father would do at home. Books will begin to be a familiar part of the children's background. They will like being read to and they will enjoy looking at the pictures.

There are other activities that will go on in the classroom from time to time. Examples of such activities are: woodwork, playing with puppets, and playing with puzzles and games. There will also be very lively current interests continually cropping up. For instance, there may be a visit of the circus to the neighbourhood; or a Harvest Festival service in school; and all the activities of Christmas will always arouse a spontaneous interest that we can use as a basis for reading. Physical education and music, too, are pleasurable experiences that will add many new words to the child's vocabulary. By providing the right sort of environment, we are giving the child the opportunity to mature as a person, as well as fulfilling our narrower purpose of bringing him nearer to the threshold of reading.

Chapter 3

DEVELOPING CLEAR SPEECH

SOME of the poor and inaccurate reading of older children is due to poor and slovenly speech. A child whose speech is not clear may suffer from a speech defect, and when this is the case it is often necessary to refer him to the expert help of the hospital or speech clinic. Such a defect may be either physical or psychological in origin. If the child is happy, secure, and satisfied in school, a speech defect that is of psychological origin may very well disappear during the first year and before formal reading has begun. If it persists, the child needs more skilled help than we are able to give him if he is not to be hampered in the early stages of reading.

In some cases where there is no actual defect, slovenly speech habits will have been learned before the child comes to school; and of course, the influences that have led him to acquire these habits will still operate after his school life has begun. Such children can be helped to speak more clearly during the preparatory period. Through talking about their play, young children will learn to speak more clearly as well as to use language with meaning and precision. They unconsciously imitate the adults who are closest to them, and by talking to them about their play we can help them to express themselves in clear sentences. They will begin to copy both what we say and how we say it and in this way their spoken language will improve.

Stories also can help. Young children like stories in which the characters are familiar, and the events such as might easily happen, or almost happen, to them. They like stories with plenty of repetition, such as *The Three Bears*, or *The Tale of a Turnip*, and they like to hear the same stories told over and over again. They will begin after a time to know the stories by heart, and they will not hesitate to tell us if we make any changes or leave any part out. So the words of familiar stories will gradually be incorporated into the child's vocabulary and they will tend to be spoken as he has heard them spoken by us.

This use of words from familiar stories is also apparent in the children's dramatic work. If they dramatize the stories they have heard, they will unconsciously use some of the words from the original story. Much of their dramatic play will be spontaneous and centred on the dressing-up box, and during the creative period they will imitate the things that they see mother and father doing in the home. Both the dramatization of stories and free dramatic play will be of use in helping their speech.

Nursery rhymes and jingles will also help to get the spoken vocabulary clear. We should not try to eradicate all traces of the dialects that give character to speech, but we must correct slack and careless speech habits. Such habits will make difficulties when the child begins to read, as what appears in print may not correspond at all with the child's own auditory impressions. Wrong hearing and wrong speaking are often not apparent until the child begins to write. Then he may write "the smornin" and other phrases that show us he has been speaking carelessly. Speaking verse and jingles and nursery rhymes will help to correct this wrong speaking.

Every opportunity that we take of talking to our children, both individually and in groups, will indirectly help their speech. We can show them picture books or large pictures and let them help to explain what the pictures are about. We can discuss the specimens that are brought for the Nature Table and the plants that are growing there, as well as the models that have been made and the pictures painted in the creative period. In these situations, and in many others that will arise spontaneously from day to day, we can help the child to speak clearly and to increase his command of spoken language. In so doing we shall be helping to give him the tool of clear speech, without which he will be handicapped as he begins to learn to read.

Chapter 4

READING THROUGH INTEREST

THE child has no natural impulse to learn to read. Reading is a skill that the human race developed late, and if we are to help the child to acquire it, we shall need to be aware of the innate impulses that each child possesses in varying degrees, since these can be the driving force as he begins to acquire the skills of reading, writing and number. He has a natural impulse to imitate adults. He is self-assertive, and he is by nature curious. His desire to imitate will make him want to learn to read and write as he sees his parents, his teacher, and his brothers and sisters doing. The impulse of self-assertion will want to make him succeed, and his innate curiosity will give him an attitude of wonder and interest towards much that he sees going on around him.

In the initial stages of reading, we try to follow the emerging interests of the child. We need to be sensitive so that we follow his real interests, and not what we imagine that these interests should be. Here, our knowledge and experience will provide us with some guiding principles that apply to many children.

We know, for instance, that most children are interested in events in their own lives, in their homes and families, in things that they themselves make, in living and growing things, in listening to stories, and in new experiences that come to them within the secure environment of the home or classroom. It may not be easy to discover the interests of the shy, slow or difficult child, but play in the kind of environment we discussed earlier in Part I will help him to reveal his interests to us.

Subject only to the well-being of the classroom community, the child will for a considerable part of each day be allowed free activity within this carefully planned environment. His tasks will be self-chosen. By watching him at his play and seeing which activities really hold his interest, we shall be guided to provide him with the right reading material.

7. Reading a wall story about the home interest. Five-year-olds match first the sentence and then the phrase to the original story

8. Reading arising from playing at 'mothers and fathers'

It is a good plan to provide some sort of reading material as soon as the children come to school. So many of them come in a mood of keen expectation. They think that they are going to learn to read and write and do sums, and it can be a real disappointment to them if they are made to engage in what they call "play" all day. So, for those children who want it, and perhaps are ready for it, let us provide some simple reading material. This could be in the form of a simple sentence written in large script on a big sheet of paper saying,

"We have started school this week"

The children can then "read" this sentence. This reading will at first only be repeating the sentence with the teacher, but if they can do this the keen children will not feel disappointed. These children should also be introduced to the Book Table and given access to paper and pencil so that they can "write" if they wish.

The following are some ways of approaching reading through interest.

1. *Free drawing or painting leading to the writing of individual or class news*

It is often by painting or drawing that the child first tries to put his thoughts into visible form. Most children by the age of five years, if given access to suitable material, will want to draw or to paint. Usually, when we have gained their confidence, they will want to talk about their drawings, their paintings, or about the model they are making. It is upon such lively interests as these that we shall base much of our earliest reading material.

When the children have settled into school and have got used to handling brushes and paints and crayons, we give them each a news book. Not all of them will be ready for this book at the same time; and those who are not ready, or whose manipulative skill is poor, will go on painting and drawing on large sheets of paper or blackboards. These children may meet their first reading material through the class news sheet, or we may put a big label on their painting saying,

"David painted this ship"

They will not in any way be given a feeling of failure if they are not quickly able to use a news book.

D

The news books should be large in size. A page that is twelve inches long and ten inches wide is a satisfactory size to begin with. These books can be made from kitchen paper if they are not included on the requisition list. Books of the exercise book size are not big enough for this purpose, as children of this age will not have acquired the fine muscular control that is necessary to use them satisfactorily. The drawing and writing may be done either with thick greasy crayons or with beginners' pencils.

At first the children will draw in the books, being told to use only one page at a time. While they are doing this the teacher will go from child to child, listening to what they have to say about their drawings. When the children have got used to drawing in this way, the teacher suggests that she should write under the picture, telling what it is about. This writing should be as nearly as possible in the child's own words, as these are the ones that he will remember. So at first he may ask us to write:

"*My baby*"
or "*Me and my mummy*"

As his confidence and his command of language increases he will make sentences:

"*This is my baby*"
"*I am going shopping with my mummy*"

For a while the child may do no more than accept what we have written under his picture and remember the sense of it when he looks at the page again next day. He will have taken the important step of associating written symbols with meaning, and it does not matter at this stage if he does not remember exactly what has been written. After this, we may suggest to him that he writes with a different coloured crayon over what we have written, and in doing this he should be encouraged to write the words from left to right. When he can do this with some skill he can take the further step of copying the sentence underneath rather than over the original letters.

When they are writing news the children need considerable help from the teacher. The teacher can most successfully give the children the help they need by not having the whole class writing news at the same time. A group of twelve or fifteen children can be drawing in their news book while the rest of the class is engaged in occupations of the quieter type. The task of the teacher is to let each child talk freely about what he is drawing and then to write for him the sentence that he wants to describe the picture.

Writing in this way can provide the opportunity for some incidental teaching about the technique of writing. For instance, the sentence being written may be:

"My new baby is called Michael"

The teacher will say the words as she writes them, and when she comes to the word *"Michael"* she may very well say, "Michael, and we begin it with a capital M because it is the baby's name." She may in a similar way comment on the formation of individual letters. This teaching should be incidental. It should not be laboured so that it becomes a burden to the child. If the situation is sensitively handled by the teacher the child can begin to acquire good writing habits from the work he does with his news book.

Working with only a group in this way will give the teacher the opportunity to do some useful work with each child. As well as writing on the new page she should turn back to previous pages and help the child to remember what he has written there. Writing news in a group rather than as a whole class means that each child will add only one or two pages to his book every week and in this way he will be more likely to remember what is written on the previous pages. He will of course be free to draw or paint what interests him on the days on which he is not using his news book.

When he has been copying sentences for some time, or towards the end of the preparatory period, the child will begin to try to write his own news. This is the stage at which he will need a great deal of help and encouragement. To write in this way he will need to be able to recognize words away from their original context. In writing his sentence he will copy some words from reading material that is available in the classroom, and the rest he will either guess or ask his teacher to write on a slip of paper for him.

For instance, a child may want to write:

"I went to play in the park with my sister"

He will know the word "*I*" because it begins so many of the sentences in his news books. He will know the word "*play*" because it comes in the sentence, "*We play with sand here*" which is written over the sand trolley. He may know the word "*park*" because in the class news there is a sentence that says "*We all went for a walk in the park.*" The word "*sister*" is to be found in the reading cards that he has learned in preparation for his first reading book. These words, interesting because they mean something to him, he will have learnt to read in other contexts, and he will be able to find and copy them when he is writing his news. He will need help with the less familiar words, and with those that have no distinctive shape by which he can recognize them, and this help we can give him when we sit by him and hear about his picture.

It is worth while spending a considerable amount of time with the children who have reached this stage of news writing. It usually begins when the child is ending the preparatory period and beginning formal reading, and it is a stage at which he can easily be discouraged. If we do discourage him, then what he writes will be stilted and lifeless, and he will not progress towards vivid and lively descriptive writing.

While he is at this stage of transition between copying and writing for himself, we should be readily available when help is needed. We should also show the child how to use all the reading material that is at his disposal. Above all, we should be patient and encouraging, and to this end it is worth while sacrificing, for a short period, time that would normally be given to other aspects of work in the skills. When he is through this difficult period, during which he needs so much help, the child will begin to write stories and descriptions that are clear, spontaneous and interesting.

The class news book also has a place in the work of the preparatory period. It can be used most successfully to record news that is of interest to the whole class. Generally speaking, news that relates to one child only is best put into that child's own book. The class news book should tell of interesting things that happen in the school, such as the Harvest Festival, or the Christmas party. It may include information about class pets, or about a model that is being made. The sentences should be short, for the class news is for the whole class and should not be so difficult that many of the children find it impossible to remember it.

Most teachers find it satisfactory to have the news written on large sheets of paper and joined in some way at the top. The writing should be done by the teacher and should be in clear well-formed script. When one achieves some skill with a ball-pointed lettering pen, this writing can be done quickly and satisfactorily. Alternatively, if a crayon is used the news can be written at once instead of being added later as it must be if a pen is used. There will usually be many volunteers among the children to illustrate the news.

It is impossible to say precisely how many sheets a week should be added to the class news book, as this will depend partly upon the situations that arise needing to be recorded in this way. There may be some weeks when nothing at all is added. Our school is in an area in which many of the children have not good reading backgrounds, so that for us it is a mistake to add to our news sheets too quickly. To do so is to have a news book whose contents the majority of the children cannot begin to remember. Usually not more than one or two sheets will be added to the book each week.

As in the case of the individual news books, the class news should be written as nearly as possible in the words of the children themselves. This may not be possible when the grammatical errors are too glaring, but the children will remember sentences in the form in which they, themselves, make them rather than as we may carefully change and word them. The class news sheet should be used as a tool for the direct teaching of reading. Its contents should be repeated and remembered. This need not be in any sense a form of drudgery that will destroy the children's interest in reading. Rather it can be a game in which each child has the opportunity to satisfy his impulse for self-assertion by successfully remembering sentences or words that are within his range of ability.

The children who are mentally not ready to read with a book, or who are slow even with the work of the preparatory stage, can work as a group with the class news book, using the book itself and flash cards based on it. This, too, should be approached as a game, and the children will begin to remember the words and sentences that describe happenings that are of real interest to them. Individual apparatus based on the sentences in the news book can be used as another means of ensuring that the children really become familiar with the words. News writing, using as it does the day to day living interest can be one of the most satisfying ways of approaching reading.

2.   *The wall story*

In the preparatory period the wall story may often be similar in content to the class news sheet. As he reads it the child approaches reading through sentences that are full of meaning for him. In this way it is very different from the material that we used in the early days of the sentence method. This was often in the form of verses which not only did not spring from the living interests of the child, but in many cases were not even understood by him. The wall story as we use it today is the continuous record of a story, or of classroom happenings in which the children are interested. Its continuity distinguishes it from the isolated sentences of the news sheet.

A wall story may be introduced after the children have been in school for some weeks and after they have had some experience in repeating the sentences of the class news sheet. It should not be a story that the teacher plans carefully, thinking that it should interest her class. She should be sensitive to their real interests, and these should be the basis of the wall material. Their interest in what is being said will help the children to remember the sentences. It will make them want to remember, and this remembering with interest is the first step along the road to reading.

In one of our entrants' classes the children wanted to play at mothers and fathers. They had no Wendy House in their room, and so they set about making one from a clothes horse. With the help of their teacher they painted bricks on strong paper which they nailed on to the clothes horse to make the walls. They left a space for the window at which they put curtains. In the Wendy House they put the table, chairs, doll's bed and dresser that they already had in the room. These, if they had not been part of the classroom equipment, could very well have been made. They made a rug with strips of material on a box-loom, and having put the doll's tea service and kitchen set and their dolls into the house, they were ready for imitative play.

This was obviously an interest that could provide material for a wall story. The story was written in short sentences.

"We are making a house"
"It has red brick walls"
"It has a window"
"It has curtains at the window"
"Inside there is a table"
"There are some chairs"
"There is a bed" and so on.

These sentences were written by the teacher in large bold script on sheets of kitchen paper. The children took it in turns to make the illustrations. These illustrations may either be drawn straight on to the sheet, or several children may make a picture illustrating the sentence and then the class can choose which one is to go on the wall. There will be interest and excitement in watching the story grow.

The story of the house is an example of a story that lasted over a fairly long period, but the skilful teacher can seize upon and use much more transitory interests. One morning, one of our classes went for a walk in the nearby park and the park-keeper took them into one of the greenhouses and gave them two potted plants to take home. The children were thrilled and excited about this. During the dinner hour the teacher wrote the first sentence about their outing:

"We have been for a walk in the park"

and the children drew a picture of the whole class walking in the park. The next two sentences followed quickly. They were:

"The keeper gave us two plants"
"Here they are"

In this case interest in the adventure of going out of school with their teacher was a powerful factor in aiding memory.

A well-loved and well-known story can sometimes be used to make a wall story. When this is the case, it is often possible for the story to be told verbally in such a way that some of the familiar phrases can be incorporated into the written story. *The Tale of the Turnip* (by Elizabeth Clark) could be used in this way:

"Once upon a time
"There was
"A little old man
"A little old woman
"A little girl
"A little black and white cat
"And a little tiny mouse"

Repetition of words and phrases helps the child's memory. So when he meets the words *"A little"* in one sentence after another he will begin to recognize and remember them.

When, at a later stage, the sentences are long enough to require several lines of lettering, the child will begin to develop rhythmic eye movements as he reads. When this time comes the lines should be of even length and not broken up by pictures, so that the eye can move steadily along one line and then make the backward sweep to the beginning of the next. In the early wall stories the child is not reading in this way. He is remembering sentences, phrases, and words because of their interest for him, because of their shape, and with the help of the picture. We do not, therefore, need to be so much concerned about the even length of the lines, and sentences can very well be broken according to the sense and phrasing rather than when the end of a line is reached.

It is not sufficient to provide the children with a wall story, well-lettered and well-phrased, illustrated in a lively way, and based on real interest. That is only the first step. The wall story must be intelligently used by the teacher as a basis for some direct and definite teaching. To provide the right material is to take the first step, but that material must also be used skilfully. How then shall we use our wall story? Each teacher will work out in detail her own way of doing this according to the needs of the particular group of children she is teaching. The following is a possible way.

When the first sheet is to be shown the children are gathered in a group round the teacher and they may talk freely about whatever interest the wall story is going to describe. As she talks to the children, the teacher will use the words that are on the first sheet. She can then

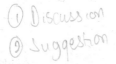
① Discussion
② Suggestion

say to the children, in the case of the story about the house, "Shall we write a story about the house? Here is the first part. It says, *We are making a house*." The children then repeat these words once or twice with the teacher, and the first sheet is pinned on the wall. By the next day the picture will have been made to go with the sentence, and this can be stuck on while the whole class watches and then reads the sentence again. Another sentence is next decided upon by the children and written by the teacher on the blackboard. On the following day the wall sheet with this sentence written on it will be shown to the children, and the next picture will be made. In this way the sheets will be introduced at the rate of about two a week, so that there is not more new material than the children can remember.

gradual build up of Story

Each day the class will read the sheets in a short lesson of five minutes or so, so that the sentences are memorized. Sometimes the children themselves are so anxious to get on with the story that the reading sheets have to be produced more quickly. The wall story should all the time be within the scope of the child of average or slightly below average ability. The child who is obviously going to be a natural reader can be given more difficult material in other ways.

The first wall story should be short, and the children may not progress beyond the stage of remembering each sentence as a whole. This story should not be discarded, but may be kept and re-read. Very soon the phrases within the sentence will be recognized and this process may be helped by the use of flash cards. These can be made so that the lettering is of the same size as that on the sheets. The cards should at first be exact copies of whole sentences. These can be shown to the children and matched by them with the corresponding sentence of the wall story. When this can be done accurately flash cards of phrases can be made and matched with the phrases in the original sentence. The last stage is the matching of the words within the sentence, concentrating at first on the significant words that have a distinctive shape.

When some children are nearing the end of the period of preparation for formal reading, we can introduce into the wall story some of the vocabulary from the introductory reading book. It is not always possible to do this, as the current interest may provide a vocabulary that is quite different from that of the book. The story of the house, in the class in which it was used, helped the children to learn many of the words from the introductory book of *The Happy Way to Reading*. Other stories can be used in a similar way, so that when the child begins his first reading book much of the vocabulary is familiar. Of course the wall story is not the only available means of becoming familiar with the vocabulary of the first book. Many reading series provide preparatory sheets and cards for this purpose. The wall story may, however, often be used to supplement this published preparatory material.

When the wall story is ended it should be made into a book and hung near the book corner where the children can still read it. Some teachers find too that the children enjoy small copies of the wall story, which can be made of manilla card and put on the book table. Individual word matching and sentence matching apparatus can be made from the words and sentences in the wall stories. So the wall story may be used in three ways: it may be read by the whole class; it may be made into a book and used by a group; it can also be used as a basis for individual apparatus which will profitably employ the children during the practice period in the skills of reading, writing and number.

Reading the wall story will continue after work with the first reading book has begun. It can very well continue in every class in the Infants' school. When many children are reading the first books of the series, those who are not mentally ready to take this step can use the wall story as their chief reading material. Short class lessons in reading the sheets will still be taken, but, in addition to these, the children who are slowest in beginning to read can work in a group with their teacher, practising and repeating sentences from the story. These lessons will be taken rather as a game than as a drill, and the smallest successes should be praised.

In one class in our school the teacher sits for this group lesson on a small chair with a blackboard resting on the floor and propped up beside her. One or two sheets of the wall story are taken from the wall and pinned to the blackboard. The children sit on a rug in a loose group facing the board. One has only to watch these children during what they call their reading lesson, to know that they are enjoying it. Sentence matching, phrase matching, and word matching go on just as they do in the short class lesson, but the pace is slower and each child in the group has a chance to take part, and to feel that he is succeeding. Sometimes this group will develop a separate interest and when this happens their reading material will be based on it. The teacher tries, without too obviously dictating the sentences, to ensure that this group which is slow to develop meets the words of the first reading book in as many contexts as possible.

3. *Reading at the book table*

There are three reasons for regarding the book table as an essential part of the classroom environment.

(*a*) The home experience of the child is supplemented by the book corner. In it he can experience the fascination of books and stories and the world of make-believe.

(*b*) Throughout his school life the child can find books on the book table that he wants to read, and that it is within his power to read. The carefully-made selection will always include books that are suited both to his mental age and to his interests.

(*c*) In the book corner the child will begin to develop the right attitude of mind towards books. In the preparatory period the child's attitude of mind towards reading is all-important. As we gather a small group of children around us in the book corner and read a simple story to them, the situation approximates to that of the family group in which stories are a joy, and books treasured possessions. We should read our children stories, and we should tell them stories that are carefully chosen and well-prepared. They will catch our enthusiasm, and be influenced by our choice of words.

(i) *The arrangement of the book table*

The amount of space that is available will be a controlling factor as we decide how to set up our book corner or book table. The term 'book corner' may be discouraging to teachers who have small classrooms, large classes, and furniture that is difficult to move. But, however difficult our situation, we can usually contrive something in which the right atmosphere can be created.

It is possible to keep the books in a number of ways. When there is a real shortage of space we can use hanging bookshelves. These are quite simply made and can be painted in an attractive colour. Alternatively, pockets can be made to hang on the sloping surfaces of a painting easel; when not in use the easel can be folded and left to stand against a wall where it will take up very little room. Pockets made of strong material can be made to hang on the wall. These are all improvised storing places.

For rooms in which there is more space, furniture can be bought for this purpose. A wooden book-screen is a satisfactory place for housing a small number of books. A wooden book trolley has the advantage of being easily moved to any part of the room. On it we can keep books satisfactorily and display them attractively. For the preparatory stage, when the books are relatively few and often changed, some teachers prefer to use a spare small table.

In whatever way we may decide to keep or store our books, the place in which the children sit to read them must be as attractive as we can make it. The use that the children make of the book table will partly depend upon how attractive it looks. There will be no irresistible attraction in a neglected-looking orange box filled with dirty, old and tattered books. The book table needs constant attention if it is always to look fresh and inviting. This need not be an additional daily task for the teacher. The children can take their share in caring for it.

However crowded our classroom may be, it is well worth while trying to create a feeling of quiet and privacy for the children who are reading in the book corner. A clothes horse, covered with cotton material that can easily be removed and washed, makes a most satisfactory screen for this purpose. Placed between the children who are reading and the rest of the class, it will shut them off from the many attractions and distractions of the other part of the room, and it will help to suggest quiet. When not in use it can be folded and put out of the way.

Inside our book corner we shall put a few children's chairs. If there are no spare chairs the children can bring their own when they come to read. Generally speaking, about six is the maximum number of children who can use the reading corner satisfactorily at one time. If the classroom is furnished with desks, two of these can be pushed together so that their tops join to make a flat surface. This surface should be covered with a clean and attractive cloth made, if possible, from similar material to that on the clothes horse screen. If a table is used instead of desks, it too should have a table cloth and a vase of flowers that is kept always fresh, and is of such a shape that it cannot easily be overturned. We shall all find our own way of planning our reading corner so that it looks attractive, and so that it fits into the pattern of our whole classroom.

(ii) *The choice of books*

Our choice of books for the book table will be guided by the age, the interests and the mental abilities of our children. In every class there will be a considerable range of mental ability, and a great diversity of constantly changing interests. This is true of a class in which the chronological ages of the children are roughly similar. These differences and diversities are, of course, much greater in classes where there is a difference of one or two or even three years between the youngest and the oldest child.

In considering the books that we shall provide, it is always the reading age of our children rather than their age in years that must guide our choice. Thus, in the entrants' class at the end of one or two terms in school, there will be some children who are only ready to look at picture books, to talk about them with us, and to listen to simple stories that we read. There will be in the same class some children who are able to make a fair attempt at reading by themselves a very simple book of the type that has one sentence on each page. A few children may be capable of more than this. The book table must supply books that are of the right degree of difficulty for each stage.

An intelligent three-year-old may sit on his mother's knee and revel in the words and the rhythm of *Bad Sir Brian Botany* or he may be fascinated by *Winnie the Pooh*, and even begin to remember whole stretches of the familiar and much-loved dialogue. This is the beginning of the right feeling for books, and the child who has an experience like this is fortunate. If the books are worn and have been used by his brothers and sisters before him, if they are kept in a special place and taken down and read as a great treat, he begins to know that they must be treasured and treated with care.

Unfortunately, many children are given by their parents unsuitable books of the 'annual' type, or others that are of poor quality in every way. The print is small and not clear, much of the subject matter is remote from their real interests, and the pictures are badly drawn and crudely coloured. Small print and difficult subject matter may sometimes be acceptable in the books that are read to children as distinct from the ones that we provide at school for them to read for themselves.

It matters very much what sort of books the school provides. The teacher will have some that she keeps carefully in her cupboard. These she will read to the children, showing them the pictures and building up an attitude towards books similar to that fostered in a good home. As well as these, there will be the ones in the book corner.

These need not be elaborate or expensive. In the past the number of suitable published books was small. There is happily an increasing number of such books, and a list of some of them will be found at the end of this book. They should be attractive to look at, the pictures should be clear and in good colour, and the print should be of fair size. They should either be strong, and be able to stand up to much handling by little children, or if they are less durably made the worn copies should be frequently replaced.

Some of the books, especially during the first term, should be of pictures only. Coloured photographs or well-produced pictures of known objects and familiar happenings provide the opportunity for talking that some of our children need. They should be encouraged to talk to us about these pictures, so that they become increasingly able to express themselves in coherent sentences.

Other books should contain pictures each with a simple sentence underneath. This sentence should be closely related to the illustration so that the child who is used to looking at the picture, and talking about it, takes the next step of accepting and remembering the printed words that describe it. New books can be introduced in story time. The pictures are discussed and the simple story read aloud, sometimes more than once, so that the children begin to remember the words. We can then put the book on the book table, and read it sometimes to small groups of children there.

(iii) *Books that can be made*

During the preparatory period we shall almost certainly find it helpful to make some of the books ourselves. In this way we can follow up any

A book made by the teacher for the children in the preparatory stage

activity that interests either a group of children or the whole class. If any child is absorbed in an interest or phantasy of his own we can make a book that is primarily for him. Often there will not be a published book that is suitable.

The children will enjoy helping to make these books. They will bring pictures and will be able to help with cutting them out and sticking them in. They can suggest the wording that goes under the pictures, and, because they have joined together in expending time and effort to make the books, they will all be the more likely to care for them and respect them.

We can make these books in a number of different ways. The material used should be durable or the pages will quickly tear, and the children will be disappointed because their effort has been wasted. We can punch holes in thick cardboard and join the pages together with coloured card or elastic. Manilla card can be used in a similar way, or we may choose sheets of strong thick paper. A paper book will last longer if the cover is made of rather thicker material. The cardboard, manilla or paper should be attractive in colour, and several different colours can be used for one book.

Home-made books need not be of a uniform shape. For a book about houses, all the pages could, for instance, be cut in the shape of a house. Similarly, books about trains or ships could be made in the appropriate shapes. Some books can be square, some rectangular or some made to open like a concertina. Some will necessarily be large, for they will be made by joining together the sheets of a wall story.

The material inside the books will be as varied as their shape and form. In some there will be one picture on each page with a descriptive sentence underneath. Some pages will contain a collection of pictures of one kind, such as a page of birds, and a page of animals or flowers. If we are making the books ourselves, we should give some thought to the lay-out of the page, the placing of the pictures, and the spacing of the writing. We shall greatly increase the attractiveness of our page if we leave margins at the top and bottom and on each side. Any well-printed book will illustrate the pleasing effect that results from the right use of margins.

For the lettering a ball-pointed lettering nib is easy to use, and it produces clear script of an even thickness. We can use any waterproof ink or paint that does not smudge, provided that the colour contrasts sufficiently with that of the paper to show up clearly. The following are some suggestions of books that the teacher can make. Many more will arise from the special interests of each individual class:

Things I can do, A book about boys, A book about girls, Hymns we know, Poems we like, Things that help me to grow, A book about the Zoo, My book of animals, Things we do in school, Games we play, My family, A Thank You book, A Christmas book, A book about holidays, A book of shops.

4. *Reading arising from the centre of interest*

In the preparatory period the centre of interest is of a less permanent

9. In the reception class reading material may be based on a current interest

10. The junk table as a basis for reading with children aged 5 to 6½ years

nature than it is at a later stage. There is seldom one for the whole class. Rather, there tend to be many activities in which the children are engaged. Some of these will hold the interest of a group of children for several weeks. Others may absorb their attention for only a few days. Sometimes the introduction into the classroom of a new pet or a new toy will interest the whole class.

There will be interests that come and go, but that of playing at homes and at mothers and fathers is common to most children. The appeal of this sort of play will be stronger for some children than for others, but most of them possess the impulse to imitate the behaviour of loved adults. This impulse may lead to other kinds of imaginative play, but for many children it finds its outlet in domestic play.

This means that there should be in the entrants' classroom some sort of home corner. Here, for the first weeks in school the children will play freely, cooking meals, laying tables, making beds, taking the baby out, going shopping to imaginary shops and doing all the other jobs that they have seen their mothers and fathers do. At first they will play alone, or in small groups, but gradually they will begin to play together in larger groups. One child will be "Mother," one will be "Father," and there will be the baby and various other members of the family.

When the play reaches this stage, some reading material can be introduced. If the introductory book of our reading series tells of the activities of a family, the material arising from the home interest will be an invaluable preparation for it. In our school we use *The Happy Way to Reading* so our home corner becomes "*Tom Bell's house.*" The children, as they begin their play, hang labels round their necks saying either "*I am Mother*" and "*I am Father,*" or "*I am Mrs. Bell,*" "*I am Mr. Bell,*" "*I am Joan Bell.*" Thus the vocabulary of the first reading book gradually becomes familiar by being used in play situations.

Playing at homes leads quite naturally to playing at shops. The shopping play may in the beginning be entirely imaginary. The child will go to a certain place in the room and pretend that he is shopping, and he will not feel the need for any external aids to his imagination. When play of this kind persists, the teacher can suggest that a shop is introduced into the room. At first it is likely that this will be a general store. It can be very simply set up and given a name. Articles to sell

E

in the shop can be made in the creative period, and a list of things that are for sale can be made.

In addition there will be a notice saying:

"Come and buy at our shop"

and there will be notices saying when it is "open" or "closed." Sometimes the interest in shopping grows and the children want not one shop but several of different kinds. When this happens the scope of the reading material is naturally widened. Each shop will have its own name and its own price list. This is the sort of development that does not come in the first term in school, but rather at the end of the first year, or at the beginning of the second. Shopping play and home play can each provide the material for a wall story.

The domestic interest is the most common and the most lasting one, but there are others that arise from time to time and that can be used with advantage as a basis for reading. Some of these last only for a short while. An interest of this kind may be seen when the school is preparing for a harvest thanksgiving service. A sheet can be prepared saying:

"Next week
"we shall have
"a harvest service"

This can be followed by another which says:

"We shall bring
"these things"

Then will come sheets on which the teacher writes the names of all the fruits and vegetables that are brought, and on which the children draw them. The gifts as they are brought can be gathered together and labelled, either with their name, or with a sentence saying who brought them. During this week it is often convenient and suitable that the nature table should become the harvest festival table. Words that will frequently be met in reading, and sooner or later needed in writing news can be learnt in this way.

In one class a group of boys was particularly absorbed in floor play with bricks. This interest developed when the class took its creative activities into the hall. Here, there was plenty of space and play with a train set could be incorporated into the imaginative play with bricks. Soon the children were building roads, stations, bridges, tunnels, houses and fields. The farmyard animals and trees were introduced into the play, and model cars were brought to put on the roads.

This play persisted over a period, and the teacher wisely devised some reading material around this interest. There was a short wall story about a train which the group learnt to read, but the most valuable material was that which the children used in their play. This consisted of labels that could be used with the model as it was made. There were names of stations and labels for houses and bridges, and these of course were put in different places as the model was differently built each day.

It is possible for an absorbing activity and a wall story to be used as valuable aids to reading independently of each other. Although in practice it very often happens that the activity provides the opportunity for the making of a wall story, with young children it does not always do so, but can, nevertheless, provide a valuable basis for reading. The children will use labels and notices in their house or shop or model, and in their news books they will begin to try to write about their play.

5. Reading arising from nature interests

The nature table should in the widest sense be a focal point in every classroom where there are young children. Children will not only be interested, but they will experience a sense of wonder as they care for things that live and as they watch things that grow. Even at the preparatory stage much reading will arise from these interests.

The most common form of reading material is the label that identifies the flower or leaf or twig. These labels can all too easily stay on the nature table for so long that they cease to be noticed. If they are really to be of use they need to be collected regularly and put out again in their right places. This can be done as a game, sometimes by the whole class and sometimes by a group. Collecting the labels also means that it is easier to keep the table fresh and well cared for, as the opportunity can be taken to dust it and throw away dead flowers.

In one class the labels were so made that the children could replace them correctly without the help of the teacher. Made of thick manilla, they bore on the front the name of the flower, and on the back an actual specimen, pressed, and secured behind cellophane. The making of these labels took time, but no one going into that particular class would have doubted that these children were interested in their nature table.

It is also a good idea to label specimens that the children themselves bring, with a sentence:

> *"John brought these shiny conkers"*
> *"Diana found these bluebells in the woods"*

Here again, the labels should not just be put on the table and left there, but the children, especially the ones who brought the specimens, should be encouraged to read them.

There can be other, more general, labels introduced in connection with the nature table at the preparatory stage. The children will be particularly interested in watching the progress of things that grow. If they have planted beans there can be a series of labels appearing at the appropriate times:

> *"Watch our beans grow"*
> *"There is a white root"*
> *"The leaves are beginning to grow"*

Similar reading material can arise from planting grass, or mustard and cress, or anything that will not take too long to germinate.

Young children like to see things happening, and their interest is most easily aroused by plants that will grow quickly. This does not mean that they will not enjoy things like bulbs, but that their lively interest in watching something sprouting in a very short time can be used in helping them to learn to read about what they are seeing.

Five-year-olds will delight in caring for the nature table and a chart may be made showing them who is to do this job each day:

> *"Please tidy the nature table today"*
> *"Peter"*
> *"Susan"*

The sentence can be written on a sheet of manilla card and the names inserted into slots underneath. In this way the children will not only learn to read the sentence telling of this job to be done, but they will have a real incentive to begin to recognize their own names. Charts may also be made, telling who is to care for any pets that there may be in the room.

"Please feed the goldfish today"
or
"Please look after the guinea-pig"

Notices may also be made listing the food that the various pets like to eat.

"Our guinea-pig likes to eat these things,
carrots,
apples,
lettuce"

Occasionally the nature table may be used to show all the things that a particular pet eats. In one of our classrooms where there is a guinea-pig there was a label over the nature table saying:

"Brownie likes to eat these things"

and on the table with their appropriate labels were a lettuce, some apples, some carrots, and a saucer of milk.

In another class of five-year-olds, Sally, the guinea-pig, became at one time the centre of interest. Wall sheets with illustrations were made saying:

"We have a guinea-pig"
"Her name is Sally"
"She lives in a box"
"She makes her bed of hay" and so on.

The children, in their first term in school, were really interested in reading the story of Sally.

Reading arising from nature interests can be of four types. There can be word or sentence labels; there can be duty charts; there can be records of growing or living things; and there can be a wall story, arising from a nature activity that interests the whole class.

6. *Reading arising from the weather chart*

Another activity that is closely linked with interest in nature, and which the children enjoy is the keeping of a weather chart. In the pre-reading period this can be very simple. A most satisfactory chart can be made from a piece of wood or very thick card roughly two feet six inches in size. Hooks are screwed into the chart, and on these are hung cards giving the day, the date, the month, the weather, and a picture of the day's weather. These cards are changed every day, and the children will often watch the weather and change the card which says "It is raining," or, "It is sunny," once or twice during the day.

An interesting weather chart

There are many interesting variants of this kind of chart. One teacher hinged together two empty picture frames of the same size so that they would stand quite steadily on a table or window sill. One of these was backed with plywood and into it were put hooks on which to hang labels as in the case of the chart described above. In the other empty frame was suspended a swing. Jennifer, a doll made from balsa wood, sat in the swing. In a box were Jennifer's clothes, a mackintosh for wet weather, a woolly jersey and skirt for cold weather, a cotton frock for sunny weather. So as well as recording the day, the date, and the month, this weather chart had cards saying:

> "*It is wet*
> "*Jennifer wears her mackintosh*"
>
> or
>
> "*It is sunny*
> "*Jennifer wears her summer frock*"

This quickly captured the interest of the children and they had little difficulty in remembering the sentences.

7. *Some other ways in which reading may be approached through interest in the preparatory period*

It is impossible to give a comprehensive account of reading of this sort, for it will vary from class to class and from term to term. Unlike the news book, the wall story and the book table, such material is not an essential part of the preparation for reading. It arises from time to time, either spontaneously or when the teacher decides that a particular class is ready for a particular piece of reading material. The following are some examples.

(*a*) *Action cards.* These are short sentences, written by the teacher on manilla or thicker card, giving certain instructions:

> "*Stand up*"
> "*Sit on your chair*"
> "*Clap your hands*"

The children read the cards, and obey the instruction. These cards can be used as a game either with a group of children or with the whole class. The children will learn to read the cards because they want to be first to do the action that is required. It is possible, of course, to ask individual children to read the cards and to perform the action while the rest of the group watches, eager to see if it is done correctly, and ready to do it themselves if it is not.

Another type of card is the one that the teacher holds up, or gets a child to hold up, when there is to be a change of activity in the classroom.

> *"Five minutes more"*
> *"Begin to put your work away"*
> *"Please stand by the door"*

It is a good plan not only to hold these cards up and to ask the children to do as they say, but quite frequently to ask them to read them aloud.
(*b*) *Classroom labels.*   There was a time when it was the custom to fix a label to every window, door, cupboard and piece of furniture in the Infants' classroom. These labels were left in position for whole terms at a time, and after they had been fixed for a week or two the children ceased to notice them.

There is a value in having such labels in the classroom from time to time. Words like *"window"*, *"cupboard"*, *"door"*, *"table"*, and *"chair"* are ones that the child needs to know. He will want to use them in his news, and he will find them sooner or later in his reading book. Like the labels on the nature table, these, too, need to be collected frequently and then put back again, as a game in which the teacher holds up a label and asks the children to show her or tell her where it goes. In this way they can be used to some purpose and they will soon be recognized and read.

Labels of a slightly different kind also have a place. These can show, first of all, where in the classroom the varying activities will take place. Examples of labels of this kind are:

> *"Play with sand here"*
> *"The reading corner"*
> *"This is Tom Bell's house"*
> *"The nature table"*

Like the labels on furniture and parts of the room, these should be frequently read.

It may not be practicable to collect them and put them in place again, but they can be read, and words from them can be found in other parts of the room. For example, when the game is being played of putting the classroom labels back in their right places the teacher, when she comes to the word "*table*", can ask the children where in another place they can find the same word. They will find it in the label "*The nature table*", and so they will begin to recognize words out of their original context.

Children's work may also be labelled. The label may be a general one, as, for example, one over a row of mounted paintings saying:

"*Here are some of our paintings*"
or "*We like to paint*"

Individual children's paintings may also be mounted and labelled:

"*This is Mary's house*"
or "*Tom painted this motor car*"

Models that the children make in clay or plasticine or waste material may be treated in the same way. There can either be a collective label saying:

"*We have made these things*"

or there can be small ones for individual models.

Most teachers will, in practice, alternate between the two ways of labelling. Generally speaking, the collective label will be of greater interest to the whole class than the individual one. There will be times,

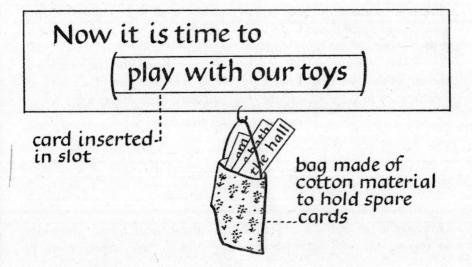

Now it is time to
(play with our toys)

card inserted
in slot

bag made of
cotton material
to hold spare
cards

though, when one child's model or painting captures everybody's interest, and that is the occasion for the individual label or caption.

In one of our classrooms was a piece of apparatus that was not strictly either a duty chart or a label. The children used it with obvious enjoyment over a period of several terms. In a place that was easily reached by the children, was fixed a long strip of card, with the beginning of a sentence written on it. The words were:

"Now it is time to"

and there was a slot at the end into which cards could be slipped. Underneath hung a bag, in which were many possible endings to the sentence.

"play with toys"
"have our milk"
"say our prayers"
"go into the hall"

At first the teacher made a point of asking children to change the cards every time they were going to do something new, and she made sure that they did it correctly. Later, whenever there was a change of occupation someone quietly went and changed the card. When a piece of apparatus of this kind is first introduced it is often quick children who use it. When it has become thoroughly familiar, it ceases to be a challenge to the more able children, and the slower children, having gained confidence through seeing it day after day, begin to use it successfully.

(c) *Charts of classroom duties.* These charts will tell the children about the duties that are performed regularly in the classroom. They will, of course, vary in the course of the year, but some typical ones are:

"Please give out the milk today"
"John"
"Mary"
"Please look after the flowers"
"Tom"
"Joan"

During the several short periods that the teacher gives every day to reading the wall material with the children, and helping them to remember it, the sentences on these charts will be read, and words from them compared and matched with words in other parts of the room.

(*d*) *Reading arising from games.* Some valuable reading material can be introduced arising from well liked games and activities. The following is an example: during the creative period the children play quite freely on the floor with bricks. Later in the day, when the activities are more specifically concerned with learning or preparing to learn the basic skills, there is play with bricks again. This time a pile of cards is put with the bricks, and on each card is a different instruction:

> *"Build a tall tower"*
> *"Build a house"*
> *"Build a big bridge"*

To help the children, a drawing of what is to be built is put by the sentence.

Very soon, they are able to read the instruction on the card as soon as they pick it up, without reference to the picture. The teacher can word the sentences in games of this kind to include much of the vocabulary that is already being presented to the child in other reading material in the room, or which will be found in the first reading books. This use of the same words in several contexts proves to be a valuable aid in building up a reading vocabulary.

These are only some of the ways in which, during the preparatory period, reading can arise from the natural interests of the children. The ways of approaching reading that are of the most constant value are the writing of news, the wall story and other reading material based on the centre of interest, and the book table. In the first two of these the reading material can meet the needs both of the able and of the less able children. It can unobtrusively be guided by the teacher, who can ensure that each child not only progresses, but progresses at the right speed. It can most truly be said to arise from the children's own interests. The third main approach to reading is the book table, for it is here that, even in his first year in school, the child's desire to learn to read is fostered.

Chapter 5

PREPARING FOR FORMAL READING

In any class there will be a wide range of mental ability. No teacher can discover immediately what is the intellectual capacity of each child in her class. Nor can she know at once whether the home environment and the developing character traits of each child are of a kind that will help him to make full use of his innate abilities. For the child, the preparatory period is one of adjustment and level finding as well as a time of widening experience and interest. For the teacher, it is a time for observing and assessing, as well as for providing the right environment and guiding the children in their use of it.

In a town school a group of forty or so children may begin school on the same day. The first five years of their lives will have been spent in widely differing home conditions. As well as this, some will be the only child in the family and others will have watched or joined in the occupations of older brothers and sisters. Some will have advanced mentally beyond the average, and others will have been slow to develop.

The classroom environment will provide for the differing needs of all these children. It will widen the experience of children from unprivileged homes. "Only" children will be able to play with others. All children will play with their contemporaries, which is a different experience from play within the family group. There will also be the opportunity for each child to work to the level of his own ability. In the first weeks, the reading material will be for the whole class.

Before long the teacher will find that some children are much quicker than others at remembering this material. She must see that these children do not monopolize the short class reading lessons and she will praise the slower children for much smaller successes. In short, the teacher will soon discover within her class a group of children who are ready to go ahead quite quickly with reading.

The preparatory period provides the opportunity for this group of children to progress as quickly as they are able. They will work as a group with the teacher. They will proceed from remembering the sentence to flash card work in recognizing sentence, phrase and word. They can work with individual apparatus that gives them practice in this phrase and word recognition. They will soon want to try to write their own news and they may be encouraged to look at and to read, first with the teacher, and then alone, the very simple books on the book table. Before long they will be led by the teacher to reading the first books of the graded series. In this way, the children of superior mental ability will progress at their own rate, and will not need to wait until more of the class is ready.

The whole class will continue with all the approaches to reading through interest. They will all continue to read the news sheet or the wall story, to put labels on the nature table and to work with action cards, and so on. At these times the teacher will make certain that everybody has a chance to feel successful. In addition, the children who are progressing more quickly will work as a group with the teacher at a separate time.

The first group may be ready for a reading book while the next group has only reached the stage of recognizing phrases and words, and the rest of the class is still recognizing whole sentences. So it will go on until a small group of children is left who cannot handle the preparatory work with sufficient confidence to be ready for the first reading book.

The group of children who, by the end of their first year in school, have not begun to read with a book, will not have developed that attitude of resistance and disinterest towards reading that is characteristic of the older backward reader. They will not have struggled day after day with the same dirty, dog-eared page of the first reading book. They will have been introduced to books in an attractive way. Even if they have not been successful, they will have realized that written and printed symbols tell us about things that are interesting to know.

Assessing reading readiness

It is necessary to find a way of judging a child's readiness to read the first book of the graded series. Some authorities say that when a child reaches a mental age of six years he is ready to begin formal reading. This is probably true, but it is possible to find a simpler way of judging a child's reading readiness than by finding his mental age.

We can give the children a variety of informal reading material. We can let them become thoroughly familiar with the idea that written symbols convey meaning, and then observe carefully each child's reaction to the reading material with which he finds himself surrounded. We let the children who show obvious ability work more intensively as a group for a short time each day, and then we introduce them to the printed material that is preparatory to the first reading book. At this point we begin to keep a careful written record of their achievement, and when they are really confident with the preparatory cards and can recognize about 15 or 20 words away from the original context, we judge them ready to read the first book with a good chance of being successful.

After a few weeks there may be another group who are ready to do the work that is directly preparatory to the printed book. With these children we shall work rather more slowly. Again we shall keep detailed records of the words and phrases that they know.

There may very well be in the class a large group of average ability which after a while will divide quite naturally into two or three smaller groups. These children, both when they are working with preparatory material and when they begin a book, will need to tackle smaller amounts of reading, and to prepare much more slowly and carefully. As with other groups, we shall consider them to be ready for the first book when they can recognize 15 or 20 words out of their original context.

We shall be left with a small group of perhaps 6 or 8 children who, at the end of a year in school, or having reached a chronological age of six, show little sign of being ready to begin to read a book. Some of them, if left to develop at their own rate and not made to feel that they have failed, will quite suddenly be ready to read and be successful in doing so. In a few, progress may still be very slow throughout the second year. This problem of the "slow starters" will be dealt with in more detail in another chapter.

PART II

READING WITH A GRADED READING BOOK

WHEN the first group of children is ready to begin to read the first book of the graded reading series, we need to find ways of organizing the teaching of reading so that we can keep the right balance between the more formal and systematic side of the work and the approach through interest which is so important throughout the child's life in the Infants' school. The work of the second year, when all except the very slowest children begin to read the graded series needs to be considered and planned very carefully. At this stage most children need a lot of help from the teacher, and the work of the day must be planned so that she is available to give this help, for it is vital that at this point the children should not fail and be discouraged.

Chapter 6

CHOOSING A SERIES OF READERS

THERE are many series of reading books available, and our choice will be guided partly by the needs of our particular school, and partly by our own views and preferences. It may vary according to the home background of our children. If many of them come from privileged homes where they are helped and encouraged to read, our main reading series can be one that progresses quite quickly. If, on the other hand, the home environment for the majority of the children is poor and lacking in any interest in reading, we shall choose a series in which the first books at least do not present difficulties that are likely to be discouraging.

We shall, if it is possible, have more than one series available. Whatever our circumstances, whether ours is a country school or a town one, whether our children are fortunate in their environment or whether they come from homes that are less privileged, there are certain qualities for which we should look as we choose our reading series.

1. *Subject matter*

In the first place, the subject matter should be suitable and of interest to the children who are to read it. This means that the first books of the series should tell of people and events that are familiar, for young children are interested in people who are close to them, and in happenings that are within their own experience. For most children the familiar environment is that of home and school, the people in whom they are interested are those whom they meet from day to day, and the happenings that concern them are those that form part of their own life.

So the first books of the reading series should tell the story of the ordinary life of children in an ordinary family. They should describe the things that happen at home, the games that the children play, the people that they meet, how they go to school and what they do there. This is familiar, secure ground and its appeal will be general.

11. A group of six-year-olds who are slow to begin formal reading, use reading material arising from a centre of interest

12.   An interest in shopping may provide much useful reading material for children at the end of their first year in school

This does not mean that in choosing reading material we ignore the children's imaginative play, and the phantasy life that is often so real to them. A child may go through a phase when, for the time being, he literally is a ship, or a Red Indian, or a Cowboy. He may have an imaginary companion who is sometimes just as real to him as any of his family. These interests, which are often individual, find expression in the child's painting and in his creative writing. Sometimes they are shared by several children, and if this is so the group will have a "centre of interest" in the true sense of the words. Certainly we shall base reading on interests such as these. They are however, peculiar to individual children, or to groups of children, and therefore they do not provide such suitable material for a series of reading books as do the people and situations that are within the experience of most children.

If the subject matter of the reading book is of this familiar kind, there is a natural link with the play interest of the preparatory period. The spontaneous playing at mothers and fathers can lead to playing at being the family in the reading book, so that there is the link which we try to make on every possible occasion between reading and the child's natural interests.

The choice of a reading series may be guided in some measure by whether the children live in the country or the town. Town children may be ready to read about farms and the country by the time they reach the third or fourth book of the series, but material of this sort is not the most suitable for the first books. The converse, of course, is true of country children. Between the ages of six and seven, as they progress through the reading series, the children's interests and experiences are widening all the time. This should be reflected in the subject matter of their reading books. As their interests develop so the range of suitable reading material extends. The last books of the series should contain some well-known fairy stories told in simple language. If this is the case, reading with his reading book will gradually become for the child the same thing as reading stories for pleasure. If the stories are worth while and the language carefully chosen, the first step will have been taken towards developing the child's literary taste.

2. *Range of vocabulary*

Thinking of the language that is used leads quite naturally to the

F

second point that we should consider in choosing our reading series. We should try to find one in which the vocabulary is carefully chosen and controlled. The choice of words will of course depend very much upon whether the book makes a predominantly sentence or phonic approach. The relative merits of these two approaches to reading, have been set out in Chapter 1.

If the majority of the words used in the first and second reading books are ones that can be "built" phonically, the resulting reading material is likely to be stilted, unnatural and lacking in interest. If, on the other hand, we are going to ask the child to read short sentences about familiar events, and well-known characters, we must be certain that we are not expecting him to remember more words than he is ready for. The vocabulary of the first books needs to be systematically planned. There should not be too many new words on each page. For the first few pages one sentence on a page is enough, and there should be repetition of words and repetition of phrases from page to page.

It is a help to the teacher if new words are listed beside their page number at the back of the book. This enables her to see at a glance which are the new words on any page, and thus time is saved in preparing new work. These lists of words are not necessarily to be read painstakingly by each child before he passes on to a new book. Children vary in their ability to recognize words out of their original context, and it is the experience of the teacher, rather than the exact number of words read, that will help her to judge when the time for a new book has come.

The first two books, then, need only a few new words on each page, these should be often repeated. The good series provides sufficient repetition without being dull. A small amount of reading material on each page means that the child will get the feeling of achievement that comes from successfully reading a page and turning over to a new one. This experience can be taken one step further if the first books of the series are short, so that there is also the achievement of finishing one book and going on to the next.

The feeling of pleasure that comes with success as he begins to read is important especially for the average and below average reader. If he likes reading he will be ready to co-operate with us as we try to help him through the more difficult phases. The child will be the more likely to like reading and to gain confidence if his reading vocabulary increases at the right pace and in a planned way.

3. *Illustrations*

It is a natural progression to pass from thinking about vocabulary to considering the pictures with which the book is illustrated. They need to be considered both artistically, and from the point of view of helping the child to read the text. Not all the pictures with which our reading books are illustrated are equally successful in helping the child to read. But it is possible for the picture on each page to illustrate the text so closely that the child, with a minimum of help from the teacher, reads the correct words. This close co-operation between the artist and the writer is particularly desirable in a series that uses the sentence method.

The child at first relies on remembering the sentence, and a picture that helps to recall the exact sentence is invaluable. To achieve this result the illustration must be clear and bold, avoiding distracting and fussy detail. The books we give children to read in school will be helping to mould their taste, not only from the point of view of their subject matter and literary value, but also through the artistic merit of the pictures with which they are illustrated.

Many of our children see in their homes, books that are a part of the great mass of badly presented and artistically poor material that is produced for children. Unconsciously, children will accept the standards with which we present them at school in this connection. One of the things we should look for in a reading series is that the pictures should be good both in line and colour.

Not only should the pictures be good, but the whole book should be attractive and well-bound. Children cannot satisfactorily be led to care for books that are so poorly bound that they fall to pieces with only normal wear and use. Children like books that look attractive and whose covers show the different books in the series quite clearly either by colour or pattern.

The print should be of the right size for the children to read comfortably. Broadly speaking, young children need larger print than older children. Their eyes have not yet developed the fine control that is necessary for reading small print easily. So the first books of the reading series should have clear and well-spaced print. The books that are to be read by older children may have smaller print, but the pages should not be broken up by pictures interspersed in the text, as these interfere with the rhythmic eye movements that are necessary for fluent, easy reading. The pictures should be either at the top or at the bottom of the page, or on a page by themselves.

4.   *Apparatus*

Individual and group apparatus can be used with the reading series, and in choosing a series we should look for one that has suitable published material of this sort. Types of apparatus that are most generally useful are flash cards, word and picture matching, and reading and doing cards of all kinds. Modern methods demand thought and hard work from the teacher. Much of the material that she provides for her class is suitable for that class only and could not be found in any printed or published form.

Chapter 7

ORGANIZING THE MORE FORMAL TEACHING OF READING

1. *Introduction*

When one or two groups of children are ready to begin reading the first book of the carefully chosen graded series, we must consider how we can best organize the teaching of this more formal aspect of reading. Each teacher may need to plan according to the size of her classroom, the size of her class, and the age or ability range of her children. Looked at broadly, the situation is similar for all of us.

In every class there will be a group of children of superior ability who are ready to progress very quickly; there will be a large group of children of average ability who need to go more slowly; there will be another smaller group who, although they are below the average will, nevertheless, be able to make some attempt at reading; and there will be a very small group who may meet with very little success while they are in the Infants' department. For all but the first of these groups, learning to read means acquiring a difficult technique. We have to decide how best we can help these children while still retaining their interest and confidence.

Our aim should be to hear them read from their books every day. In the early stages this is desirable for two reasons. When he begins to read his book the child is remembering rather than reading in the fullest sense of the word. He will be helped to remember accurately if we can hear him read and refresh his memory every day. Secondly, he likes to feel that he is "getting on" with his book. He will be the more successful in doing this if we can hear him and help him each day.

Even after the first book or two books have been read the children are still very dependent upon the teacher. They learn to read by reading, and by far the most profitable reading they do is reading aloud to the teacher. They still need her encouragement and her help with new words, and the more often she can find time to hear them, the more likely they are to progress with their reading.

The only exceptions to this daily rule are the fluent readers. These children may need little help and can be left to read by themselves for the sheer enjoyment they will get from doing so. They can keep lists of the books they have read, and the teacher should hear them read from time to time so that they learn to read aloud fluently and with expression. They should also be asked to write about, or to tell about the stories that they have read, so that we can be sure that these have been understood.

When they begin reading books and when they are experiencing some difficulties, we should try to hear our children read every day, and one of the greatest difficulties that a teacher experiences is ensuring that the rest of the class is profitably occupied while she is hearing reading. This is a problem that taxes our ingenuity and our powers of organization to the full. It needs to be considered, firstly from the point of view of our actual method of hearing reading, and secondly with regard to the kind of work that the rest of the class can do.

2.   *How to hear reading*

(*a*)   *Class reading.*   There are three possible ways of hearing children read. We can hear them as a class, we can hear them in groups and we can hear them individually. Few people nowadays seriously consider class reading as being a psychologically sound method of working. In any Infants' class the range of mental ability will be so great that there must inevitably be a large group of the children who not only would not profit by such a procedure, but who would suffer more harm than might appear immediately and superficially.

If the reading material were suitable for the middle group in the class, the children who were above average, even though they might appear to be attending, would be developing an attitude of boredom and apathy towards reading. The slowest children, even though their eyes might be upon their books, would be experiencing the feeling of discouragement and failure that go into the making of backward readers in the Junior school. There can be no justification for the class method of teaching reading.

(b) *Individual reading.* To hear children individually seems to many teachers to be the right method. They hold that each child has his own difficulties and progresses at his own rate, and that therefore he needs individual attention. This may be a matter of personal opinion. Some teachers sincerely feel that given ideal conditions and a small class the individual approach is the right one. Most of us however do not work in ideal conditions, and our problem is that we have to deal, not with a small class, but with large numbers of children. We need to find a method that will enable us to give them an adequate amount of time and help as often as possible.

A concrete example may help to make the situation clear. If it takes a minimum of three minutes to hear one child read and to prepare the new work with him, it will take twenty-four minutes to hear eight individual children, even if one does not take into account the time taken for one child to return to his place and for the next to be ready to read. A group of eight children can be heard quite satisfactorily in little more than half this time, which makes it possible to hear them twice as often. To hear reading in groups is a satisfactory and convenient way of giving the children the daily help that they need. It is also true that many children are definitely stimulated and helped by reading in this way.

There are some exceptions, and some situations in which it is desirable to hear children read not as a group but individually. The first group of children in any class to begin reading with a book will be the most able readers. These children will experience few difficulties, and can with profit be heard as a group.

With the least able children a slightly different method may be necessary while they are reading the first books. They can work as a group with the teacher in preparing a new page. They can also work in this way with flash cards in the practice lessons that will help them to recognize the words and phrases from their book. But when they actually read the page in their reading book, it is often helpful while they are on the first one or two books to hear these children read individually. This means that they will come to us alone with their books and we shall hear them and give them the help that they need. This group of children will keep on the same page or pages of their books, they will work as a group in preparation and revision, and when they begin to be established and to build up a reading vocabulary for themselves they will be ready to do their reading as a group.

The third group of children who may not need daily group reading are the older able readers who can read any simple book with little help from the teacher. These children can read alone and be heard occasionally. They will also enjoy reading stories aloud to the class, and should have definite training in doing this. If they spend too much time in silent reading they may slur over their words and pronounce them incorrectly. Training in reading aloud for the pleasure of those who are listening will help the quality of the reading of all who are at all fluent. In most classes the reading of the rest of the children can be heard in groups.

3.   Group reading—its advantages and disadvantages

The term "group reading" can mean different things to different people. What is meant in the present context is that reading is taught in the following way. Towards the end of the preparatory period a group of from six to ten children will emerge who are obviously ready to read a book. The reading ability of these children will be roughly similar. They will gather in a group round the teacher and talk about the reading book with her. They will look at the pictures and talk about the family in the book. They will use the pictures to help them to decide what is the story of the first pages. If they have used preparatory apparatus in connection with the series they will be able to read the first pages. The teacher will read the first pages aloud to them, and they will be excited to see how much they too can read. They will then go back to their places, taking their reading books with them and re-read the pages by themselves before they go on with the rest of the work.

When they are beyond the first familiar pages the group lesson will follow a slightly different pattern. The children will gather in a group round the teacher and she may begin by showing them flash cards of words or phrases from the page they are reading, or from pages they have already read. They will try to recognize these. At first they may need to refer to their books in order to do so, but after a time they will become quick at this word recognition.

After a few minutes of this work the children will turn to the page in their books that they are reading. They will take it in turns to read aloud while the rest of the group follows. When a page has been read satisfactorily, a new page will be prepared. This may be done by first discussing the picture and trying to imagine what the story is about. Then the teacher reads the page to the children. Having read it through so that the children catch the sense and the interest of it, she draws their attention to the new and unfamiliar words. She may have a blackboard at the children's level by her side and write the new words on it, letting the children practise trying to recognize them.

After this, while the material of the new page is still fresh in their minds, the children go back to their places and re-read it. This seems to be an infinitely more satisfactory practice than for the children to prepare a page just before the group lesson, for after a lapse of time it is possible that the text may be remembered inaccurately.

There are some obvious advantages to this method of hearing reading. From the teacher's point of view much time is saved. By grouping the children for reading, the new pages are only prepared once with the whole group instead of once for each individual child. Similarly, revision work does not need to be repeated. Time is such an important factor in the many-sided work of the modern classroom, that any method that both saves time and is satisfactory psychologically and educationally is worthy of our serious consideration.

Let us then consider the advantages of group reading psychologically, and from the child's point of view. By the time the children reach the middle of the Infants' school a definite group feeling begins to grow up. It is not until they reach the Junior school that they begin in real earnest to organize themselves into groups and gangs, but in the second half of their life in the Infants' department, children for the most part cease to act only as individuals, and the group idea begins to be acceptable to them. The children will readily accept the idea of working as a group for reading, and by working together they can help each other. If the children are well grouped this working together can be a source of help and encouragement. They will be enthusiastic and for this reason, as well as because their teacher has more time to give them, they will progress more quickly.

To summarize, the group method of hearing reading is not only to be advocated as a means of saving time in dealing with large numbers of children. It is a stimulating and valuable method both for the teacher and the child, especially if the group is not too large. Without doubt the child progresses more quickly in this way. The group will read several pages or a whole story in a lesson in contrast with the one page that is often the daily ration of the child reading individually. In short, the group method is stimulating, practicable and psychologically sound.

There are some objections that are raised to working in this way. To work the group method successfully the teacher needs to believe in it, or at least to have an open mind and to be willing to try it. She also needs to be capable, not only of handling it tactfully and with understanding, but of organizing it skilfully. The possible disadvantages can all be overcome, given the right attitude of goodwill and sensitiveness on the part of the teacher.

One possible disadvantage is that the groups may be labelled the "top group" or the "bottom group." It is merely sentimental to pretend that children do not realize that some of them read much better than others. To them this is a fact that they accept. The important and significant thing is our attitude to this fact. If we too accept it calmly, without emotion and without paying it undue attention, then the fact that one group is reading Book 3 while another is not yet "on books" will not assume undue importance. If, on the other hand, we are tempted to lose patience with the slower readers, and to threaten them with going "down a group" if they do not try harder, then we may be doing irreparable harm to their self-confidence. We may get from them a greater semblance of outward effort, but their goodwill and their interest will not be with us as we teach them to read. There is no necessity to talk about "top" groups and "bottom" groups, or going "up" or "down". Instead we can talk about "Mary's group", or "the group that is reading Book 2," or "the red book", and in this way the wrong sort of comparison can be avoided.

Another difficulty that some teachers find in working the group method is that of knowing what to do about the child who, for some reason or other, cannot keep up with the rest of the group. Such a child may have had a long absence from school, or he may be progressing more slowly than we anticipated when we first put him in the group.

If the child is a good reader and has merely got behind through being away from school, the situation presents no great difficulties. We can give him individual help, and he can be helped by other children in his group or by children who have got further with their reading until he has read the pages that he has missed and caught up with the rest of his group.

The child who does not keep up because the group is going too quickly for him may be more difficult to help. His confidence will be undermined if he feels all the time that he is limping along behind the rest of his group. If our relationship with the child is right, if being in a "top" or "bottom" group does not result in the teacher's attitude being one of praise or blame, a situation of this sort can be handled tactfully, but quite directly.

Children respond quite happily to the attitude of the teacher, which says in effect, "John, we seem to be going just a little too fast for you. I'm going to put you in Mary's group, where you'll be able to read well and to help the others." In brief, the advantages of the group method of teaching reading are that there is a very definite saving of time and that the children help each other. The disadvantages are only apparent if the teacher is not happy with the method or if she does not use it in the right way.

Groups may be used as units for teaching reading with the graded reading book and for work with the interesting books that are supplementary to their series. They may be used sometimes for approaching the other reading interests in the class room at a suitable level. This will foster the idea of reading for pleasure. It will also be roughly according to their reading groups that the children will be engaged in working with individual apparatus.

4. *Organizing the work of the rest of the class*

However we may choose to teach reading, either individually or in groups, we are confronted with the task of devising suitable individual or group apparatus for the rest of the class to use while we are hearing some children read. Many young teachers are troubled by the question of noise during this period, and they also find difficulty in providing useful work that will occupy the children who are not reading, for long enough at a time. There is no simple solution to either of these problems. The key to the successful handling of the situation is careful organization. For the teacher, modern methods are not "free" in the sense of being haphazard. The environment in which the children can be free needs to be carefully planned and thought out.

The problem of noise, especially with the younger children is a real one. No one would think of demanding absolute silence from young children while they are working individually, but a certain level of quietness is desirable if reading is to be heard in a way that is satisfactory both to the teacher and to the child.

The difficulty lies in the fact that some of the number and reading activities in which the children are engaged may be legitimately noisy in a moderate way. In the attempt to make these activities varied and worth while many teachers, while they are hearing reading, let the rest of the class do number activities, "snap" games, reading lotto, and number activities of all sorts. These are all activities with which it is most desirable that children should be occupied, if not every day, at least several times a week.

Experience in our own school has led us to the conclusion that they are not activities that can most successfully be carried on concurrently with group reading. We now take these more active and legitimately noisy occupations at a time when we are not hearing reading. We find this to be doubly satisfactory. It does not impose upon the teacher the strain of feeling that she needs to ask for a standard of quietness that, because of the very nature of the situation, is neither right nor easy to obtain. It also leaves her free to give the children the help that they need in the more practical reading and number activities. During the reading periods the children work with reading and number apparatus that they can use quietly.

Providing and caring for a sufficient amount of individual and group apparatus is not a small task. There is some published apparatus that can be used or adapted, but much of the most valuable is that which is made by the teacher to follow up the wall story, the centre of interest, and other reading interests in the room. If the reading series is well-chosen, there may be useful apparatus available in connection with it. The most difficult age group to satisfy is the one that is in its second year in school.

Both in their reading and in their use of apparatus, these children will need much help from the teacher. There are some small points of organization that help with the smooth running of the work.

It is easy, while the teacher is hearing reading, for the children to take from the cupboards work that is either too difficult or too easy. They need some sort of guide to help them to take the apparatus that is right for their particular stage. If the teacher is to give an adequate amount of time to hearing reading it is impossible for her to watch to see that each child chooses apparatus of a suitable degree of difficulty. If the children are to profit from this individual work, it is essential that they should use the right sort of apparatus.

A practical solution to this problem is to paint the insides of the cupboards red, blue, green and yellow. The colours correspond with the grading of the apparatus, and on each piece of apparatus is a coloured spot to show the cupboard to which it belongs. The children know that they are working from the green cupboard, or the blue cupboard, and they find no difficulty in choosing and changing their apparatus.

One of the advantages of the modern method of teaching is that it brings to the child's notice, in some very practical ways, the desirability of considering the convenience, and comfort, and happiness of other people. One of the ways in which this happens is in the manner in which apparatus is treated and cared for during this basic skills period. It is possible for a child, left to himself, to scribble on the apparatus and to put it away in the wrong place with some pieces missing. He may do that himself and suffer no ill effects. If, however, someone else ill-treats the apparatus in the same way, he may find that his favourite pieces of apparatus have been removed from the cupboard because they have been spoiled, he may not be able to find them because they are in the wrong place, or he may not be able to use them properly because they are incomplete. So he begins to learn that he must use the material properly in order that everyone else may enjoy it.

There are some ways in which the teacher can help the child in this right use of apparatus. She can mark it clearly with the colour of the cupboard in which it belongs. She can also, by providing rubber bands and durable boxes to hold small pieces, make it a fairly simple matter to put the piece of apparatus away complete. By careful marking she can ensure that a piece that has been genuinely mislaid can, when it is found, be restored quickly to its right place. These are all devices that help the children to care for the material that they are using. Until they are used to doing this some careful supervision should be exercised, and we should tell them why this is necessary. If we do not encourage our children to think of others in this way, we are not fully using modern methods as they can be used in helping to mould the characters of our children. At the same time we are not organizing our methods efficiently so that they work to maximum advantage.

5.   *Apparatus for the younger children*

The apparatus that the children use during the period devoted to practice work in the skills of reading, writing and number, should be of a kind that demands activity and effort. If the child takes from the cupboard a task that can be completed in a minute, it is too easy for him and he will gain little from using it. The careful grading we have discussed above is one way of ensuring that this does not happen. Another way is to consider each piece of apparatus that we make or plan, and to make certain that it requires that the child should expend some mental effort as he uses it.

For younger children "reading and doing" cards of all kinds are suitable for use in the skills period. In one class the teacher cut up some old reading books and stuck sentences from the book on to brightly-coloured cardboard. The cards were worded in the following way:

> *"Draw and write*
> *'Here you see all the family'"*

The sentence would be one that the child had actually met in his reading book. He would meet it on the card in the form in which it was familiar (or in the actual print from the book), but he would meet it without the picture to help him to read it. Some of these cards only ask that the child should,

> *"Draw*
> *'This is Tom Bell'"*

and when this is the case the card needs to be numbered and the number

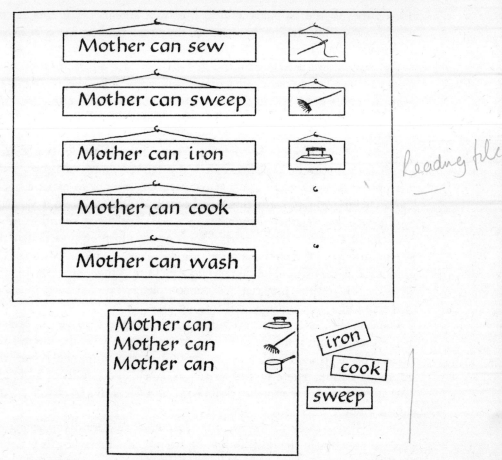

Reading file

"Reading and doing" cards

copied by the child into his book so that it is a simple matter for us to check the correctness of his drawing. This is only one simple example of how the material of the reading book can be used. There will also be apparatus that can be bought with the reading series, and all of this is valuable in that it presents the child with the vocabulary of his reading book in a different way, thus helping to impress it upon his memory.

This driving home of half-familiar vocabulary through attractive and interesting occupations is a great help to the child. Much of the apparatus that he uses should be purposeful in this way, and should follow up the vocabulary of his reading book or of the other reading material in the classroom.

The wall story especially can, and should, be used as a basis for individual work. The wall story only half achieves its purpose if the sheets are merely read through by the whole class from to time. It should be the "reading book" of the slower readers, and "reading and doing" cards should be made for use in conjunction with it.

In one of our classes the story of "The Three Bears" appeared in a simple form upon the wall. Later, it was mounted on manilla card, holes were punched in the card and a cord threaded through to make a book. The matching phrase cards that had been used with it while it was still on the wall were gathered together in a box. For many months one or two children would take out this book every morning and match the phrase cards with the phrases on the original sheets. Sometimes one of the more able readers would be there to hear them read the sentences. As time went by this reading material became completely familiar even to many of the children who did not find reading easy.

The centre of interest can provide reading material that we can present in the form of apparatus in numerous ways. Here again, the interest has already been aroused and may be centred in the shop, the house, the seaside or station. There will be price lists, labels, and notices of all kinds. The apparatus uses a similar vocabulary, and the driving power of the child's interest helps him to remember the words.

This carrying-over of interest from the creative period to the period devoted to work in the skills should be attempted whenever it is possible. It can be a powerful factor in helping the child to read and to write and to count. It is not enough to give the child a rich environment in which he can create and experiment. We should try to let the driving power of his play interests influence and vitalize all that he does during the rest of the day. An example of this carry-over of interest can be seen in the children's play with bricks. During the creative period they will play quite freely with the bricks. During the practical period of noisier reading and number activities they may play with bricks again, but this time we shall give them reading cards to use with them. The cards will tell them, for example, to:

13. The first stage of writing news. The child writes over the sentence the teacher has written at his request

14. The second stage of writing news. The child copies the sentence that the teacher has written

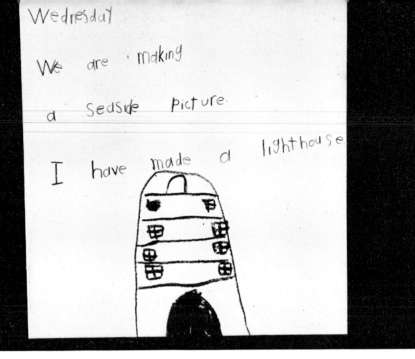

15   The third stage of writing news. The child begins to write by himself

16.   A later stage in writing news. The child writes more, and expresses his thoughts with increasing facility

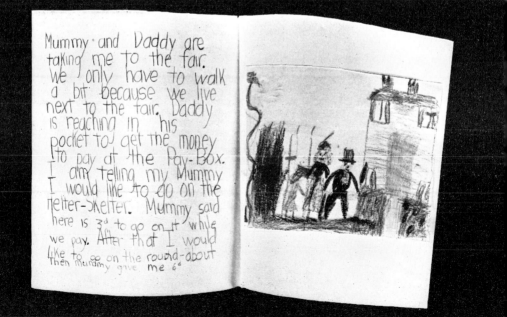

17.   The hospital as a centre of interest with children aged 6½ years

18. Two centres of interest at the seven-year-old stage

> "*Make a house*
> "*Put a garden round it*"

During the quieter period of work in the skills they may take these cards from the cupboard and use them as 'reading and doing' cards. With a little help they can learn to change the sentences to:

> "*I made a house.*
> "*I put a garden round it*"

and they can make a drawing of the house and the garden.

6.   *Hearing reading 5½ to 6 years*

How shall we organize our class of 5½ to 6 year-olds during a "basic skills" period in which we hear reading? First we set the whole class to work with reading and number apparatus. The group that is to read first gets its books ready and gathers round the teacher. In some classes the teacher sits on a low chair and the children on a rug in front of her, or the teacher sits at her table (which she has taken care to clear of all the odds and ends that collect there) and the children stand round the table resting their books upon it. In other classes, where the children are sitting round three or four tables that have been pushed together to make one big table, the teacher hears reading sitting with the group at their own table.

The group lesson proceeds while the rest of the children work with apparatus. When all the children in one group have finished reading and have prepared the new page, they go back to their places and read the new work through by themselves while it is still fresh in their minds. Afterwards, they work with apparatus.

The teacher then asks the children in the next group that is to be heard to get their books ready and to read through their page quietly by themselves. While they are doing this she goes quickly round the class, so that all feel that she is interested in what they are doing. Perhaps she will comment on what is being done, or encourage the children who are working slowly. She may help, where help can be given quickly; she may see that the maximum effort is being expended, or she may make a note of situations that require more detailed help at another time. After

G

five minutes or so spent in this way she will hear the next reading group, and the whole process is repeated.

This method works well with children in their first year of learning to read. These children for the most part are not yet able to work for long periods by themselves. They need a variety of occupations, help, and approval. By going round the class after hearing each group read, we can be sure that apparatus is changed as often as necessary; we can often give help just at the right time so that the less able children do not become bored and anti-social; and by our encouragement and approval we can help the children to put forth their maximum effort.

Sometimes with these younger children it is a good plan to break off this skills period after hearing perhaps two groups read and to take a short, five-minute class lesson. A number rhyme can be taught and played, or we can do some word or phrase-matching with the wall story, or play a game with action cards. After a brief spell of being organized, and of working as a class the children return readily to the individual and group work.

By hearing reading in groups in this way, it should be possible to hear each group read four or five times a week. This is particularly desirable during the first year of reading. In this year, if the child is ready to read he will be able to progress quite quickly. We should try to provide him with many opportunities for reading, not only from his book, but with apparatus, and from wall material.

7. Suitable apparatus for the later stages

During the last year in the Infants' school, the wide range of mental ability that is to be found in any class becomes apparent in the progress that the children have made in reading. At the beginning of this year, the natural readers will be reading quite fluently from any of the simple books with which we provide them, while the least able children may not yet have begun to read with the graded series. Between these two extremes there will be four or five or six groups, all at different stages. In such a situation the apparatus will need to be carefully graded, for the performance of the children will vary greatly.

The lowest group of children will still be using apparatus similar to that used by the rest of the class in the earlier stages. They will need

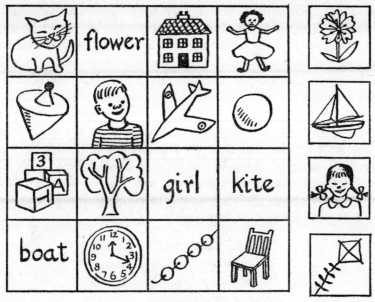

Reading lotto

simple reading and doing cards based on familiar material, word, phrase and sentence-matching cards, simple word games (such as "lotto" and "snap") and self-corrective apparatus, of all kinds.

This apparatus, although similar in type and in degree of difficulty, should, if possible, not be the identical material used in the previous year. Slower children need the stimulus of attractive new apparatus, which should be devised in connection with the current centre of interest. Material that is preparatory to the reading series will naturally be less varied, but even here we should try to give the less able children new apparatus from time to time, with the necessary vocabulary presented in different ways. Apparatus that is attractive and carefully graded, and not grubby, drab, and over-familiar, will help to keep alive their interest and will foster their desire to read.

Many of the reading interests in the later stages will arise from the centre of interest. For the able children, reading and creative writing go hand in hand at this stage, and they will often be engrossed for long periods at a time, needing only the minimum of guidance from the teacher. These children may read library books in connection with the main interest, and then reproduce the knowledge so gained in simple books of their own. They will write stories and diaries, and read book after book, and our problem is not to occupy them during the skills period, but to find the time to read and correct the great mass of material that they produce.

The children in the middle groups will, however, need some help and guidance if they are to make the best use of their time. For these children cards that set a definite task are most suitable. Some of these may arise directly from the wall story. In one of our classes where there was a model of a Post Office, there was on the wall a poster showing: "How the mail is delivered in the Highlands". In connection with this poster was a reading and doing card which said:

> "*Read the poster about*
> "*the postman in the Highlands.*
> "*Write a story about him*
> "*Make a picture*"

Other cards based on the Post Office interest said:

> "*Buy a birthday card from the shop*
> "*Buy an envelope*
> "*Buy a stamp*
> "*Post the card in the pillar box*"

Many examples of this kind could be given. The value of apparatus of this sort is that most of the words and phrases on the card are already familiar, that the subject matter is of interest, and that the child is presented with a definite task to be done. We can also use the reading book as a basis for apparatus of this sort. Questions can be asked about stories that have been read, and by this means the teacher can find out whether the children have understood stories that they have read by themselves.

It is suitable, too, that some individual apparatus should be made to give the children practice with phonics and word families, and even in the last year in the Infants' school there is still a value in apparatus that asks the child to match words in one way or another. The child can become familiar with new words from centres of interest, nature tables, and wall material in this way. Many pieces of apparatus can be devised on the same lines as "lotto" for this purpose. These can either be used by the children individually, or two or more can use them as a game.

Much of the apparatus that the children will use in this period is neither completely reading apparatus or definitely number apparatus, but is rather a combination of the two. A great deal of that used with the Post Office project was of this kind: many of the cards asked the children to buy stamps at the Post Office or the Stationers shop, and then to record what they had bought:

> "*Buy*
> 'One 4d. stamp
> 'One large envelope
> 'One birthday card
> 'Write down how much you spent.' "

The child would then write;

> "*I bought*
> "*One 4d. stamp*   4d.
> "*One large envelope*   2d.
> "*One birthday card*   3d.
> ——
> "*I spent*   9d.

Reading and number occupations can well be mixed during this period and practice sum cards should be available for the children to use.

8. *Hearing reading in the later stages*

In the top classes of the Infants' school, hearing reading and organizing the work of the basic skills period is in some ways a less formidable task than it is at the $5\frac{1}{2}$ to $6\frac{1}{2}$ year-old period. A group of children (and this group will vary in size from district to district and from school to school) will be able to read fairly fluently and with little help from the teacher. Most children at this age, too, are able to work by themselves with apparatus for longer than the six-year-old. This means that the "skills" period runs more smoothly. The children have acquired a habit of work, the atmosphere in the room is peaceful and everyone is engrossed and busy.

In broad outline the method of hearing reading will be the same. At the beginning of the lesson we shall set the class to work. Many of the children will be given a quota of work for the morning:

> "*Try to do this work this morning*
> "*1 shopping card*
> "*2 sum cards*
> "*1 'read and do' card*
> "*Write in your diary*
> "*Practise your reading*
> "*Write a story or read a library book*"

We can arrange this "quota" so that the first items on it are those that most of the children can do. The slowest and least able children will not reach the stage of writing a story or reading a library book.

Those children who have read the whole of the graded series, or who can read any simple book with little difficulty, will not need to read aloud every day. They should be well supplied with library books and supplementary reading books and allowed to read by themselves, only reading aloud to the teacher once or twice a week. Sometimes they can read a story to the whole class. During this last year the time that is saved in this way can profitably be used in helping the slowest readers. This is especially necessary if there is to be a change of approach and method in the Junior school. In hearing the middle groups read, we shall use a method similar to that described earlier in the chapter for the younger children.

Because they can work for longer periods by themselves, the children who are using apparatus and doing their quota of work will need less help from the teacher at this stage. Even the children who can manage best by themselves, however, will be helped by a word of praise, or some guidance given just at the right time.

For the teacher of older children, there is not the same urgent need for a quick look round the whole class that there was lower in the school, but she will be well advised not to sit in her chair hearing reading for the whole period, however peacefully and busily occupied her class may seem to be. We can encourage good habits of setting down work while the children are actually working; difficulties (e.g. in number) can be seen and corrected; and the slowest group will always be in need of direct individual teaching and help.

At all ages, the use of this wide variety of apparatus requires careful planning and meticulous keeping of records. In the later stages, it is important that the child should realize that the work he has done in his "quota" has been read, and appreciated, and in some cases corrected. In this way his interest and enthusiasm will be maintained.

Chapter 8

WORD ANALYSIS AND THE TEACHING OF PHONICS

MOST teachers who have had experience of teaching young children to read would agree that, with the possible exception of a few natural readers, they eventually reach a stage at which they need some help in tackling new and unfamiliar words. The point upon which there is a difference of opinion is not whether this help should be given, but when and how.

Our language is not predominantly phonetic, and to begin to teach reading by teaching phonics is to make a mechanical approach, and to confine ourselves to teaching words that are not those most frequently used by the child. The phonic approach does not make use of the child's known ability to recognize the shape of words, phrases and sentences, nor does it harness his interest as a powerful force in helping him to learn to read.

A reading series using the sentence approach will have a vocabulary that is built up gradually, and the words will be repeated in many contexts. The child, therefore, will not need a tool with which to tackle new words while he is reading the first books of the series, for the new words will be added gradually, at a rate at which he is able to learn them.

At about the middle of the second year, many of the children will be reading books in which the new words come quickly, and they will be ready for help in dealing with them. This is the stage at which they need definite teaching both in phonics and word analysis.

This teaching will be given at a different time from the group reading lesson, although of course the ability that the child acquires in reading unfamiliar words will be used as he reads his graded reader. The skilful teacher will help him to use this developing ability as he reads his book, in such a way that he does not lose all the advantages that have come with the sentence approach.

When about half the class have read Books 1 and 2 of the graded series, many simple supplementary books, and a good deal of 'classroom' material, their reading vocabulary of words recognized at sight will be considerable. It will be large enough to form the basis for lessons in word analysis to help them tackle new words. Moreover, they will be reading their simple books fluently and with understanding. This habit of reading for meaning will play its part in speeding up the recognition of new words, once the children have been given some lessons in word analysis.

These lessons should be short, frequent, and concentrated. For the first half term there should be one a day. After that only a small section of the class may need daily practice and for the rest one or two periods a week will suffice. At first the lessons can be for the whole class, as the material is new for everybody. The children will absorb it and apply it at different rates.

The few natural readers may not need this lesson, and if they do join in they should not be allowed to take a very active part at the expense of the less able children. At the other extreme, there may be a few children who are not yet capable of profiting from instruction of this sort. During this ten-minute lesson these children can be using individual apparatus.

Some ways of approaching word-study

The aim of all this work is to help the child first of all to analyse and then to synthesize new words. In tackling a new word, the child must be able to analyse it into its known parts and then build these parts into a whole. The larger the units he can use as he does this the simpler will the process be. With practice he will learn to deal with new words quickly, so that the flow of his reading is not impeded. The following are some ways in which we can help him to analyse new words.

(a) *The use of phonics.* Single sounds should be taught through families of familiar words. For example, in learning the letter 'b' we may begin with the word "*baby*", which appears in the reading book, and then ask the children to suggest some more words that begin with the same sound. We shall write these on the blackboard or on a large sheet of paper, where the children can refer to them easily. They can very well learn these sounds two or three at a time. They will follow the same procedure with such double sounds as sh, ch, sp, tr, bl and so on.

Phonograms will be learnt in a similar way, through families of familiar words. Some may begin, for example, with the word "read" or the word "high" and let the children suggest more words with the letters "ea" or "igh". Even the least able children will often be able to suggest words for inclusion in these lists.

The teaching of phonics should not be a long and arduous process. It can be done fairly quickly, remembering that a knowledge of phonics is only a part of the knowledge that the child needs in tackling new words.

(*b*) *Breaking words up into known units.*   The larger the unit that a child can recognize the more easily will he build a new word. So we shall teach him as he looks at a new word to find in it groups of letters that he already knows. There are a great number of words that can be analysed in this way:

> e.g. th—ink,   sp—end,   mat—ch,   sh—red.

These are words that could be sounded out phonically using single and double sounds, but the child will read them much more quickly if we can train him to see the small known words in them, and to read these as units.

(*c*) *Breaking up words into two or more smaller words.*   The idea of looking for the known unit can be extended to looking for small words, many of which could not be phonically sounded. Examples of this kind are:

> anyhow   downstairs   sometime
> underground   understand   everywhere   likeable

The teacher can suggest many words of this kind and write them on the blackboard. After some practice the children will enjoy suggesting words that can be read in this way.

This work can be taken a step further by writing a long word on the board and then seeing how many shorter words can be found in it.

e.g.   hippopotamus, in which are the words
       hip   pop   pot   am   us
or   grandmother, in which are the words
       grand   and   mother   moth   the   other   her   he

A game of this sort will help the children to form the habit of making the analytical approach. The children themselves can often suggest suitable words.

(d) *Using apparatus based on word-study.* The more difficulty he has in reading, the more practice a child will need in word analysis. Apparatus can be used to give him practice at his particular level. Sorting occupations are suitable for slower children who can sort words into families according to their initial sound, or put into groups those that have a double sound or phonogram in common. "Snap" games and "lotto" can be made at different levels of difficulty.

A rather more difficult piece of apparatus is a collection of ladders drawn on paper, on the top rung of each is a word with a certain double sound or phonogram.

e.g. *sh*—op   *t*—*ell*

The children have to supply words with similar sounds to write on the other rungs of the ladder.

Many pieces of apparatus of a similar kind can be devised for use by those children who need much practice. The more able children will enjoy making their own word books with collections of words having sounds, phonograms or other parts in common.

Word analysis should not be so laboured that it becomes a burden either to the teacher or to the children. Much of the classwork can be done as a game, taking care that the slower children have every chance to take part. Our aim should be to help every child to analyse new words with such speed that his reading becomes increasingly fluent.

Chapter 9

THE CHILD WITH SPECIAL DIFFICULTIES

EVEN though we plan our work with imagination and understanding, and we study each individual child with care, there will still be a percentage of children in each class who find more than normal difficulty in learning to read. These are the children who, after two of their three years in the Infants' school, show little aptitude for reading, and have made almost no progress. They may not have reached the stage at which they can begin to read the graded series, and may still be doing the simplest work of the preparatory period with no very obvious success.

These children will have fared much better in the modern school than would have been the case in a school that made a formal approach and expected a child to attempt to read a book before he was mentally ready. They will not have learned to dislike reading and to develop an attitude of resistance towards it. A child in this slowest group cannot help knowing that many of the children in his class show more aptitude for reading than he, but this fact will not have been stressed. His reading lesson will be with the last wall story that has been made into a book. It will often be in the form of a game, and his smallest successes will be praised. He will not need to read every word in the wall story book correctly before he goes on to "read" another similar book. Thus, there will be some variety in his reading in a way that there could never be if he were daily confronted with the same page of a too-difficult reading book. Best of all, he will not be called a member of "the bottom group", but of the group that is reading "our book about trains"—or whatever the wall story book may be.

Having provided a suitable environment, we still need to study the child carefully to find out why he is so slow in beginning to read. There are several factors that may play a part, either singly or together, in causing this slow start in reading. We can check upon the more obvious of these fairly easily.

A common cause is absence from school. It may be that the child has suffered from a succession of infectious illnesses, or he may have spent several periods in hospital or in convalescent homes. An able child may find little difficulty in making up the ground that is lost in this way, and the situation will be simplified for him in the modern school where the work is done in groups or individually. The slower child does not adapt himself so easily, and prolonged or repeated absences will hinder his progress.

Irregular attendance may have a similar effect, and here there is often more than one factor operating. The child who seldom attends school for a full week at a time usually comes from a home that is unhelpful in one way or another. Sometimes the home life is so erratic that the child has to stay at home to help, or is too late to come to school. Sometimes the parents are so over-anxious about his health and well-being that he is kept at home unnecessarily. Whatever may be its cause, the child whose attendance is broken and irregular does not settle down into that steady, secure rhythm of school life that helps him to make good progress. Often when we look closely at the attendance record of the children with difficulties in reading we find that it is unsatisfactory.

There are other situations in the home that can affect the child's performance at school. Jealousy of a younger brother or sister may cause him to be emotionally disturbed. An older brother or sister who has done well, and who is held up as an example may inhibit him. His father or mother may be over-anxious or over-strict. Or there may be disharmony at home so that his security and peace of mind are destroyed. Some of these causes of difficulty can be removed when once they have been discovered; others are beyond our sphere of influence, so that we can only use our knowledge of them to increase our patient understanding of the child.

To every child a feeling of security is important. This sense of security can be affected not only by irregular attendance and by emotional disturbances having their origin in the home, but also by too many breaks in the continuity of his school life. The present time is one in which many young families may move their place of living several times in the attempt to find more satisfactory conditions. For the child this means changes of school and resultant changes of method, books and companions. Even if he stays in the same school, staffing difficulties make it not unusual for a class of children to have to adapt themselves to several different teachers in the course of a term. The child of limited intelligence is slower to adapt to new conditions than is the more able child, so that it is likely that breaks in the even flow and continuity of his school life will affect his reading.

Physical factors too may cause apparent backwardness. A speech defect will make it difficult for a child to read. It will, if it is a serious one, make it difficult for the teacher to hear if he is reading correctly. It sometimes happens that the child who appears to be slow has an unsuspected defect of sight or hearing. He may be suffering from malnutrition coming from unwise feeding, or he may be getting insufficient sleep because of unsatisfactory home conditions. There is also, of course, the child with such a marked personality difficulty that he needs the specialized help of the child guidance clinic. The full energy of such a child seldom flows into his school work.

We should study our slow reader to see if any of these factors are operating, either singly or together. It may not be suitable or possible for us to do anything materially about the adverse conditions that are affecting the child. We can, however, attempt to make him secure and happy in school, and give him every opportunity to develop to the limit of his ability.

It is not always easy to decide how best to help the child, who, at the beginning of his last year in the Infants' school, has made no start upon the first book of the reading series. We have to make up our minds whether to let him continue the work of the preparatory period until he is ready for a book, or whether to give him a book in any case and "push" him through the first books of the series.

If all teachers in the primary school were equipped to teach the beginnings of reading, then undoubtedly such a child should be left to progress at his own rate. So often it happens that the child passes to another department, where his teacher has not been trained to teach the early stages of reading. When this is the case his difficulties are increased. He feels that he has failed because he is not "on a book". It is this feeling of failure that we seek all the time to avoid for the child with special difficulties.

If we know that in the next department the approach through interest is not made, and that the child will have to begin formal reading with a teacher who, however good her intentions, is less skilled than we are to help him, we may find it expedient to adopt the second-best course of helping him with his first books before perhaps he is really ready. His progress through them will be slower than it would be if we could afford to let him delay this step, and we shall need a great deal of skill and patience if he is not to be discouraged. On the whole, however, it would seem that there is less likelihood of his developing into a permanently backward reader if, in the circumstances described above, we adopt this course.

Chapter 10

STANDARDS OF ATTAINMENT

STANDARDS of attainment will vary with local conditions. The standard reached by an individual child will be conditioned, not only by his mental ability, but also by the type of home from which he comes. This is especially true of the average or below average group. The standard reached in a school will depend in part upon the type of locality in which it is situated.

In a good residential area, the level of attainment in reading will be higher than in an area where the home conditions are less satisfactory. In a school in the more fortunate type of area, the average level of intelligence will usually be higher. There will also be a larger proportion of homes that are helpful. These two factors will combine to produce a situation in which reading results should be good.

There are however other conditioning factors. The standard of reading the child reaches before he goes to the Junior school will vary with the length of time he has been at school. Not all children have three years in the Infants' department. Some are of the age for transfer to the Junior school after only two years. This depends entirely upon their date of birth, and when their particular age group was admitted to school, and the local rules of transfer to the Junior school. For all children, and more particularly for the average and slow developing child, three years is desirable. The third year is a period of consolidation during which rapid progress may be made.

Important factors to be considered are the skill and the experience of the teacher. A skilled and enlightened teacher who has a good relationship with her class will get the best possible results in her particular circumstances. A young teacher, teaching reading for the first time, will still be gaining experience, and it is unlikely that her children will reach such a high standard.

In trying to formulate a reasonable standard of attainment, let us

These are some of the
things we make with
clay and plasticine.

motor cars	clowns
battleships	cowboys
jugs	Indians
bowls	people
clocks	animals
	birds

19.   A collection of children's work used to increase reading vocabulary

20. A collection of 'Things from other countries' in a class of seven-year-olds. The labels are frequently collected and replaced

imagine a class in a school where the home environment of the children is neither very favourable nor exceptionally poor. Let us suppose that the teacher is of average skill, that she has had some years of experience, and that the average age of the children in her class at the time of transfer is $7\frac{1}{2}$ years.

The average readers in such a class should be able to read a simple story well enough to enjoy doing so. Different series of reading books are of differing degrees of difficulty, but average readers should be able to make a good attempt at reading either Beacon Book 3 or Beacon Book 4 unseen, with very little help from the teacher. They should show some power of attacking new words. If tested with the Schonell reading test, this group will score reading ages that are very near their chronological ages.

The good readers will be able to do considerably more than this. They will read fluently, and with understanding, books such as the average reader of $8\frac{1}{2}$ to 9 years can read. They will show superior ability in attacking new and difficult words. With the Schonell reading test they will score reading ages of one, two, or even three years more than their chronological age.

There will also be a group of children who are below the average. These children will be reading Book 2 or Book 3 of their graded series. They will not be established readers, nor will they yet be skilled in using phonics to deal with new words. The reading ages of this group will be a year or eighteen months below their chronological age. In the "average" class that we are considering, there will probably be three or four children who have made little start in reading. The sizes of the groups will vary according to the children's home background, as well as with efficiency of teaching.

Formal methods may achieve similar results with the top and middle groups in the sheer mechanics of reading. The natural readers will read irrespective of method. But in a school using modern methods, these children will gain far more than the skill of reading. They will have access to a great many carefully chosen books. They will be encouraged to use books intelligently as well as to enjoy them. Alongside their growing interest in reading, will be an increasing skill in creative writing. In a slightly lesser degree, all of this will also be true of the average readers.

H

With modern methods, all of these children will acquire the skills of reading, writing and number, and in addition they will be interested, alert and eager to learn.

Modern methods are also undoubtedly right for the children of less than average ability. These children need understanding, encouragement, and enlightened teaching if they are to go on progressing. They can easily lose heart, and if they are discouraged and made to feel that they have failed, they may develop into backward readers. They need continuity of method and continuity of material. If they are likely to encounter a change of both in the Junior school, it may be better for them to stay in the Infants' department for one more year, until their reading habits have been established and their confidence built up.

PART III

THE APPROACH THROUGH INTEREST WITH OLDER CHILDREN

WHEN the child begins to read the first books of a graded series, he will not discard all the reading interests that were a part of the preparatory stage. The special value of working through a well-graded series is that the child's reading vocabulary will increase in a systematic way. At the same time, many words may be learned through reading situations not directly connected with the book. The interests of the preparatory period will continue. There will still be the diary, the weather chart, the book table, the nature table, the centre of interest and a great variety of reading apparatus using the vocabulary of all these interests. The reading arising from these activities will increase in difficulty with the increasing skill of the children.

The child who acquires skill in reading slowly will still find, in the classroom, opportunities for daily experience with reading material well within the scope of his ability. Reading will not be an isolated subject; reading material will arise from, and be part of, his daily environment. He will have every opportunity to begin to read when he is mentally ready.

The reading environment that is useful to the slower child will have a value also for those who are ahead of him. Children who experience less difficulty in learning to read can be challenged by a continuation and development of the work of the preparatory period. Work of this kind can add to their reading vocabulary, increase their ability in written expression, and encourage them both to read books and to use books for reference. In the class library corner they will find a variety of books, and books will begin to play a significant part in their life in a way that would not be possible if they read only the book they had reached in their graded series. In the following pages we shall see how the work of the preparatory period develops during the later stages of learning to read, and how the methods described earlier can be employed in rapidly widening fields of interest.

Chapter 11

WRITING AS AN AID IN LEARNING TO READ

FROM the beginning, reading and writing should be closely linked. The spontaneous drawings and paintings of young children are in effect their picture writing, which they read or interpret to the teacher. They are one of their most effective means of expression before they begin to put their ideas into writing.

Making drawings of happenings within the child's experience, talking about those happenings and writing about them will begin from the first days in school, and will continue and develop throughout the child's life in the Infants' department. Children will do this work at a level suited to their own mental development.

It may well be that, in the top classes of the Infants' school, a very few children will still be copying their own news that the teacher has written in their diaries; some will be copying that and then trying to add one or more sentences of their own; while most of the class, with varying degrees of skill, will be writing detailed and lively accounts of everyday happenings at home and in school. In addition to this, some will be reproducing in their own words stories that they have heard, and some will be creating vividly expressed stories of their own.

From the point of view of the teacher, the writing of news serves a double purpose. It is a way in which children can express their ideas, first orally and then on paper. It also introduces the written form of certain words to them for the first time, in a context in which they are of interest, so that there is some chance that they will be remembered. The stages by which the power of expression in writing is acquired are as follows:

(*a*) The child translates his experience into drawing and into words as he tells us about his picture.

(*b*) The child draws, and tells the teacher what he has depicted. The teacher tries to express the child's thought in a phrase or a short sentence. She writes this and the child writes over her writing.

(c) The child draws and then copies the sentence that the teacher has written at his request.

(d) The child draws his news and then copies what the teacher has written, and tries to add one or two sentences of his own.

(e) With the aid of words supplied by the teacher, dictionaries, his reading book, and words to be found in other reading material available in the classroom (wall stories, nature table, words lists and so on), the child begins to write his own news and to illustrate it.

Some children may omit certain of these stages or pass through them very quickly. The quick child from a privileged home may be ready, after only a few weeks in school, to write his own news, helped by words that the teacher writes at his request in his individual dictionary. The slow child may stay for several terms at the stage of copying the news that the teacher writes. Each child can progress at his own rate. News writing presents the child with reading and writing, not only as mechanical skills to be acquired, but primarily as activities intimately connected with the interests and occupations of daily life. Therein is one of its greatest values in helping the child as he learns to read. The driving force of his interest can be used to help him in what is, for many children, a difficult task.

Many children will reach the stage of writing their own news by about the middle of their life in the Infants' school. At first they may only write one sentence, which, from the point of view of the adult, is neither very well written nor very well spelt, but the children themselves will experience a thrill of achievement. After that, they will progress towards writing more, and writing with greater facility.

The part played by the teacher when the child reaches this stage needs to be carefully considered. Infinite patience, a clear understanding of what she hopes her children will achieve, the ability to recognize effort, and efficient organization are all necessary in the teacher if this creative writing is to be satisfying to the child and acceptable to her. Poor organization, and a too rigid conception of what constitutes "good work", especially at the six-year-old stage, have produced results that have discouraged some teachers from experimenting with free writing. Yet all of us, having read the lucid, vivid, creative writing that seven-year-old children, given the right conditions, can produce, would wish our children to have the opportunity to develop in a similar way. There are, however, some practical problems that arise.

When he first reaches the stage at which he can begin to write his own news instead of copying what has been written by the teacher, the child needs a considerable amount of help. The teacher realizes very quickly that children vary in the amount of help they need, or are willing to accept. Some will be quite satisfied with spelling that the adult can only read with difficulty. These may be the children whose main concern is to express their ideas on paper. Ridicule of their efforts, or a rigid insistence upon correctness may all too easily check the flow of their ideas, and make their writing self-conscious, dull, and without life.

Other children, right from the beginning, will ask for help in spelling many of the words they are using. The teacher is immediately confronted by two problems. She has to decide how much she should correct the work of the child who writes a lot, but in poor writing and almost unreadable spelling. She must also organize the work of her class in such a way that she is available to the child who needs much help at this stage.

In considering how much help we should give, we must ask ourselves what we hope the child will gain from work of this sort. We want two things which may seem at first to be mutually exclusive. We want him to write freely, and with his whole heart in it, and we want him to learn the value of careful and correct ways of doing things. The one calls for writing at the speed of his thought (or as nearly as possible so), and the other calls for thinking at the speed of his manual powers.

It is difficult for the young child to concentrate upon a number of things at the same time. If he is writing about things that are real and living for him, for the time being, handwriting and spelling will be of secondary importance. In this free writing we must accept the fact that this is so.

This does not mean that we should consider handwriting to be unimportant. It should be clear and bold, and the letters should be correctly made. The teaching of the craft or technique of writing, however, should be done at a time when the child is not primarily concerned with the ideas that he is expressing. With some guidance right from the beginning, the writing in diaries and story books can be workmanlike and well spaced, even if it is not so well formed as it may be when the concentration is more upon the writing than upon what is being expressed.

1.   Spelling

Something of the same sort is true of spelling. The child should be beginning to learn to spell correctly, but correct spelling is not our first aim in this sort of free writing. A child may describe clearly and with obvious joy some incident from his recent experience. He will not continue to do so with such spontaneity if with our red pencil we correct every error in spelling. On the other hand, those of us who feel that spelling is important are not happy to leave him to make the same mistakes over and over again, so that the wrong form is impressed upon his memory.

2.   Printed dictionaries

How shall we find the middle path between correcting everything and correcting nothing? We can help our children by giving them access to as great a variety of picture dictionaries as possible, and by encouraging them to use them. Many teachers find it a good plan to set aside a bookshelf or table where the dictionaries are kept. Children enjoy finding words in the dictionaries and will soon become skilled in using them. Such work will be valuable in reading as well as in writing, for when a child has looked up a word in this way, he will be more likely to remember it when he meets it in his reading book.

3.   Children's dictionaries

Each child will enjoy, too, keeping his own dictionary and adding to it as he meets new words. Such a dictionary or vocabulary book may be made from an exercise book, indexed like an address book with the letters of the alphabet. When he wants to know how to spell a word that cannot be found either in his reading book or in the reading material on the walls of the classroom, the child asks the teacher if she will write it in his dictionary. Later, if he needs it, a small picture may be drawn beside the word by the child himself, to help him to remember it next time. We must take care that these dictionaries do not become overloaded with words that will be seldom used.

Before he can use a dictionary, the child must know his alphabet and the corresponding single sounds that will help him to look on the right page for a word. The introduction of dictionaries is a suitable occasion for teaching him both of these things. At about this stage, too, the child will have begun work on word analysis, which is an invaluable aid to spelling.

Spelling can also be taught through memory work based upon current reading interests. A sentence or phrase can be chosen from the wall story, the nature table, or the centre of interest and the children asked to learn it. After two or three days the children try to write what they have learnt. After they have attempted this they will be shown the right version, and they will correct what they have written. All except the really slow starters will be able to join in a short weekly lesson of this kind.

Even with the help of printed dictionaries, individual dictionaries, word analysis and memory work, there may still be children who persistently spell words wrongly. We can meet this problem in a simple and satisfactory way. At regular intervals the teacher can collect the diaries and read them. She can then make a list on a slip of paper of half a dozen often-used words that have been wrongly spelt. When he gets his book back, the child looks at the words on the slip, reads them himself or asks his teacher to read them to him, and then writes them on the appropriate page of his dictionary. In this way words are being added to the dictionary at a rate at which the child can assimilate them. If we corrected every mistake, the result, as well as being discouraging for the child, would be confusing because of the large number of words that might be involved.

The skilled teacher who has also a right relationship with each child will know how much effort she can rightly ask of him at each stage in his development. Some children are ready to accept correction of their work, and will even welcome it. They like to know that it is what they call "right". These children can quite legitimately be asked, for instance, to copy in good writing and correct spelling an interesting story that they have written, so that it may be put in the book corner for others to read.

The work of other children needs to be corrected very gently and very gradually, and they require a lot of praise at the same time if they are not to be discouraged. To correct his work in the right way the teacher must have some understanding of the personality of each individual child, and a knowledge of the level of attainment he has reached.

The modern classroom, in which the child can create, experiment and learn to live with other children, gives the teacher the opportunity to watch him, and to experiment with him and to talk to him, so that her relationship with him is good. In this way she can gain that understanding and knowledge of him that she must have, as she helps him to acquire the skills of reading, writing and number.

The problem of how to be available to give all the help that the children require when they are writing diaries can only be met by careful attention to classroom organization. Each teacher will work it out in her own way, according to the needs of her class and the conditions prevailing in her classroom.

If enough time is to be given to each child to make the work valuable, it is not practicable to have the whole class writing diaries at the same time. This is particularly true where the majority of the class still needs help with vocabulary or with the actual writing of the news. The most satisfactory arrangement is for a group of children to write in their diaries while the rest are engaged in work with reading and number apparatus, with which they can be profitably occupied for some time without very much help from the teacher.

It is not necessary, or even advisable, that children beginning to use diaries should write in them every day. To let them do so might mean that their individual dictionaries become filled with words at a rate which makes it impossible to remember more than a few. To write in diaries every day would also add to the difficulties of the teacher in organizing the many necessary activities in her classroom. Many teachers find that, while the children still need considerable help, it is sufficient to write in diaries twice or at most three times a week.

Children who have been writing diaries for some time, and who can do so with some facility, will need less help from the teacher while they are actually writing. These children can write stories as well as their diaries. Such stories will often amaze us by their vividness and originality. The children will enjoy reading their stories aloud to the rest of the class. When this happens we are reminded afresh of how close should be the link between reading and writing. An environment in which creative writing is encouraged and wisely and skilfully guided will be one which at the same time will help the child to acquire the skill of reading.

Chapter 12

THE DEVELOPMENT OF THE CENTRE
OF INTEREST

As the child gets older his field of interest widens. This is apparent by the end of the first year in school. In our school, when the children have been coming long enough to feel secure, they go into the hall for their creative play on one or two mornings a week. The greater space gives a wider scope to their imaginative play.

On one such morning there will be a Wendy House at each end of the hall. The "families" in these two houses dress up in clothes from the dressing up box, and visit each other, wheeling their dolls' prams with them. There is a shop where food is bought and sold quite informally, and in the middle of the hall is a group of children playing at hospitals. Sometimes one of the families will go shopping or they may pay a visit to the hospital.

In another corner of the hall is a group of children playing at schools. They have brought the blackboard from their classroom and it leans against a cupboard. One child is the teacher and the rest are the pupils. All have brought their reading books with them. The "teacher" writes a word on the board and the children find it in their books. For these children at this time play and work are closely linked.

Another group consists mainly of boys. They have brought all the bricks from their classroom, and they are using a great deal of floor space to make a large model. As well as their bricks they use model trains, small cars, farm animals and toy trees.

The children move from one group to another when they want to. They may, for example, play in the hospital for several days running, or they may move from group to group two or three times in one morning. A few children may prefer to play alone, and these are quite free to choose what they want to do from the many available occupations in the classroom.

In the class described above there are five small centres of interest operating at the same time. From each activity valuable reading material may arise. The teacher must plan this material so that there is not so much in the classroom at one time that it is confusing for the children who are slow in beginning to read.

Most of the reading material will be introduced to the whole class, and then used by the children as they are engaged in different kinds of play. All the children will be introduced to the simple labels in the shop and house. They will all begin to read the labels such as "I am a doctor", "I am a nurse", that are used in the hospital play. As they play from day to day in one group or another, they will become increasingly familiar with the material that interests them most.

Any one of these interests could provide material for a simple wall story. The most suitable ones would be the home, the shop, or the hospital, with which most children play at some time during the week. No child should feel that the wall story is completely outside his interests.

The able children can do more difficult work in groups or individually. They can make a "Book of Trains", or a "Book of Shops". In these books are pictures that the children collect, with captions written by the teacher. These children will be able to write about their interests in their news books. We can also make sure that there are simple books in the book corner, so that they can read about trains or shops or schools, or whatever their interest may be. If no suitable published books are available, home-made books, which either the teacher or the children at the top of the school can make, are a good substitute.

1. *How to use a "Centre of Interest"*

A consideration of the experience of this one class may help to clarify our thoughts. In most cases it should be an interest that comes from the children and is not dictated by the teacher. Very often it will arise spontaneously in the creative period, through a discussion, or in connection with an event in school or in the neighbourhood.

In this way a short-lived interest in puppets arose in a class in which one day a child received a glove puppet as a birthday present. Next day several other children brought puppets and announced that they wanted to make a puppet play. These were children at the beginning of their third term in school. The teacher seized upon this opportunity. Together, she and the children improvized a puppet theatre with a notice to put over it saying "Our puppet theatre". With their puppets they quite freely dramatized several of their favourite stories. They then composed a letter to the class next door inviting them to come and see the puppet show.

The teacher was quick to recognize a new interest; she gave the children the opportunity to express it, and through it she introduced them to some simple reading material. This sort of thing happens over and over again. Sometimes, as with the puppets, the interest is short-lived, sometimes it lasts over a considerable period.

Although the centre of interest springs from some activity of the children, the teacher must exercise wisdom and foresight in directing these interests into useful channels. In a class of six-year-olds where interest is beginning to widen and develop, there may be so many interests and so much resulting reading material that a child of average ability might be confused. The interests of the children can be so diffuse that they are diluted and weakened. In the classroom where there were the home corners, the shop, the hospital, the school and the floor building, this danger was realized, and the teacher kept a controlling hand upon the situation. Some reading arose from each of the interests, but one activity with a general appeal was selected for more concentrated work.

The situation sometimes arises in which the teacher can guide the interests of her children in a particular direction. There are dangers in doing this. It is easy to suggest an interest that we, as adults, think should appeal to children. At most we should suggest only a broad theme and leave the rest to them. The activities come mainly at their suggestion. The use we make of them in teaching the skills is for us to decide.

If we introduce an idea to the children, we must remember that their interest at first is in people and happenings concerning them very nearly, and it only gradually widens to include places and people and events that, although they still touch their lives, do so in a way that is not quite so close. They need to develop mentally and emotionally to a stage beyond that reached by most of our children in the Infants' school, before they are capable of being deeply interested in people who live in other countries or who lived in other times.

The centre of interest, then, is most often something that comes spontaneously from the children. Less frequently, it is suggested with imagination and understanding by the teacher. When such an interest is operating in our classroom, we have to decide what use we shall make of it.

(a) We shall try to use it as a means to help the child to increase and perfect his manipulative skill. This will happen in a number of ways. For example, the five-and-a-half-year-old making cakes for the baker's shop with flour and salt paste, or with clay, will want to mould them into the right shape and the right size. When he is seven-and-a-half his skill will have increased. He will try to make his papier mâché puppet head really look like a witch or a wolf or a bear. In his first year in school, he will discipline his fingers to weave a rug for the Wendy House on a box loom. In his last year, the stitching on his costume for the play that he and his friends are going to act will show infinitely more skill.

(b) Through the creative work of the centre of interest, the child will learn to think for himself, and to use his initiative in dealing with difficult or novel situations in construction, in the manipulation of harder materials and the use of simple tools. As he makes his train for the station that is being built in his classroom, he will give careful thought to trying to make wheels that will stay on, or that will go round. His confidence will increase if he is able to do this successfully. Only if he has tried and failed and if he asks for help, will his teacher show him how this can be done.

(c) The centre of interest, too, will lead to an increase in the child's knowledge. Not only will he learn *how* to make things, but he will learn more *about* the things he is making. In the class of seven-year-olds who were making a station, David had successfully made an engine with its coaches attached. Next, he wanted to make the lines on which the train was to run. Without any suggestion from the teacher, he took a ruler and measured the distance between the wheels, so that the rails could be made the correct distance apart. The teacher took this opportunity to tell the children about the gauges of railway lines and in this way their knowledge was increased.

(*d*) Lastly, the teacher will use the centre of interest to help the child to increase his vocabulary and to acquire the skills of reading, writing and number. Each teacher will find the way of organizing this reading that is the most satisfactory for her own class.

2. *Ways in which we can organize reading in connection with the centre of interest*

(*a*) *The Wall Story.* The most common, and in many ways the most satisfactory, form of wall story is the one that describes clearly and simply the progress of a given interest. An example of this type of wall story may be taken from a class of six-year-olds. One of the children brought from home some attractively-coloured rolls of crêpe paper. During the creative period she collected some of her friends around her, and they began to make dresses with the paper. These were dresses that they could wear themselves. After the first day, they were so delighted with what they had made that they decided they would make up a play and then make the rest of the dresses for the characters in the play.

The play was written. The children went on making the dresses. More and more children became interested and a wall story was made describing the progress of the activity. The wall story began like this:

> "*Monday, May 1st.*
> "*We are making paper dresses*
> "*Wednesday, May 3rd.*
> "*We are going to act a play*
> "*Friday, May 5th.*
> "*We have made a crown*
> "*and a wand*"

It was simply written, so that all the children could make some attempt at reading or remembering it.

The wall story need not, of course, be an account of something that is happening, or a model that is being made. It can be used to give information about the current interest. In whatever way it is planned, it should be of compelling interest, so that for this reason it will be remembered. Even at the six- or seven-year-old stage there will be some children who will be helped by having sentence cards and phrase cards that they can match to the wall sheets. These children should do this matching as a group as a part of their reading activity. When the wall story is finished the sheets can be joined together to make a large book. This book will be the "reading book" of the slowest group, and the teacher will use it every day for their group reading lesson.

(b) *Apparatus connected with the wall story.* The class as a whole will read each sheet as it is added to the wall story. The whole class will also frequently re-read all the sheets. A group may do work in matching with word, phrase, and sentence cards. There should also be individual apparatus following up this same reading material.

This apparatus should present the vocabulary of the wall story in various ways. In its simplest form it will perhaps be a small copy of the sentence on the sheet, with a simple picture to illustrate it, and with sentences, phrases or words to be matched. The child has either to put the phrases or words over the corresponding words on the card, or to look at the sentence on the card and then, with the separate words, correctly make up the sentence, either underneath the card or beside it.

Another piece of apparatus presents more of a problem. The card has written on it a copy of one of the sentences from the wall story, but there is no picture accompanying it. The child has first of all to identify the sentence by comparing it with the ones on the wall. Looking at the picture on the original sheet will help him to read it. He then has to copy the sentence and make a drawing to illustrate it. Both of these pieces of apparatus can be used by children who experience great difficulty with reading. Both of them use only the vocabulary of the original sheets. Word matching apparatus, based on the nouns in the story, is also quite simple to devise and is suitable for most children, although those who are less able will use it for a much longer time than the quicker readers. These last may only use it a few times or they may not need to use it at all.

The majority of the children in the six-year-old class who were making the paper dresses were able to use more difficult apparatus. Individual work of this kind is most satisfactory if it first sets the child a problem, and then gives him something to do. It can be used in the practice period in the skills, when the teacher is hearing reading or helping some children to write their news. In using it the child will not merely be kept busy.

21.   The nature table as a basis for reading in the reception class

22. The reading on the nature table can sometimes be centred on a classroom pet

23. The book corner in the seven-year-old classroom

The Prodigal Son.

There was a man and he had two Sons. One day he said when I am dead you will have half of all the lovely rich things. The youngest son said please can I have my half of all the money now? His father said yes. So the Son went to another Country. He journeyed two days and two nights. When he got there he bought a new house and lovely clothes. One day he had no money left so he went to live with the pigs and he ate the pigs food. At last he walked home. His father forgave him. God loves you like that father.

24.   In their last year in the Infants' School many children will either write their own stories or reproduce stories they have heard

Apparatus which demands definite mental effort will occupy his time profitably, in a way that will hold his interest and increase his ability in reading. A simple example is a card saying:

"We are making paper dresses
Draw Mary in the dress she made"

The first sentence will be known from the wall story. The second sentence has to be read and understood, and then the drawing made.

The teacher can use a simple device to find out, after the card has been exchanged for another, if the drawing is the correct one. The cards can be numbered and the child asked to copy the number on to the page with his drawing. The teacher then refers to a list of numbers and pictures that she has prepared. Alternatively, we can ask the child to write a sentence underneath the drawing saying:

"This is Mary in the dress she made"

It is not difficult to evolve more elaborate apparatus of this kind, but it should not be so complicated that it becomes remote from the interest from which it sprang.

(c) *Labels on the centre of interest.* To many centres of interest we can quite suitably add notices and labels of all kinds. The children should read these frequently and they should be encouraged to refer to them when they need words in writing their diaries.

Another class of six-year-olds made a small garden in a zinc tray in their classroom; they painted a brick wall on paper and put it all round the garden; they made paths; they made a house of wood, and they divided the garden into sections in which they planted different kinds of seeds. A notice was put over the table on which the garden stood, which said:

"We have made a garden"

Soon another was added, saying:

"We have planted some seeds in it"

Small labels were written to indicate which seeds had been planted in the different sections of the garden.

The children eagerly watched to see their seeds grow. They soon

J

knew the names of the seeds, as every day they watched each patch to see which one showed green shoots first. Then a series of short sentences were put on the classroom wall over the garden:

"The grass grew first"
"The mustard and cress grew next"

Children will read and remember labels and notices that are connected with a vital interest and in this way they will add to the number of new words that they can read or use again in writing. The most commonly used words from these labels, and from the wall stories, can be added to the children's individual dictionaries.

(d) *The children's own books in connection with the centre of interest.* The three examples (a), (b) and (c) are of reading arising from the centre of interest that is, for the most part, within the range of the slower readers. The abler child also needs to be challenged and stimulated, and we can achieve this end by suggesting that he makes his own book about the interest.

In the class that made the garden, Anthony, who was a good reader, began to make a ventriloquist's doll from junk materials. The doll was almost life-sized. Anthony made the head and face of papier-mâché. The body was a cardboard box, tightly stuffed so that it was solid, and for the legs and arms he used Vim tins. The limbs were jointed and the model was made so that it would sit down. Clothes were then made, and finally David, as the doll was called, was so life-like that at a quick glance it was easily mistaken for a real child.

For the most part Anthony made his model alone. The other children however, were completely fascinated. David became a personality to be reckoned with, and the whole class made up a song about him which was written in the form of a wall story and illustrated. They sang it to the tune of "Tommy was a soldier". Anthony, who was a quick reader, was happy enough to sing the song with the others, but he also wrote his own story, called "My book about David". In it he described how he had made David, and all the things that David could do. In this way his interest in the doll he had made furthered his interest in creative writing, increased his ability in written expression, and added many new words to his reading vocabulary.

Making books about a centre of interest need not be confined to children who can write the books by themselves. A much simpler kind of book can be made by a group of children of any age. The very youngest children can collect pictures, cut them out and paste them into a book

Barbara brought this picture of the fair.

Michael made a roundabout. This is the picture he made of it.

Pages from above made by the children about a current centre of interest

with simple captions written by the teacher. This will stimulate discussion and lead to a widening of the spoken vocabulary. Older children will have more reading matter in the book. Such a book can be a valuable aid to reading for slower children.

(e) *Collection of words.* It is often very helpful to make collections of words that are commonly used in talking or writing about any interest that is going on in the classroom. Such a collection was made in a class of six-year-olds who were making puppets. On one wall of the room was a large sheet of manilla card on which the teacher had written:

> "*We used these things to make our puppets*
>   '*Newspaper*
>   '*Paste*
>   '*Water*
>   '*Paint*'" and so on.

The children could refer to these words as they began to write their own news. The collections are also useful during the "word analysis" periods.

A class of seven-year-olds, who were making a station and thinking about holidays and the seaside, also had lists of words in their room. They had "Words about the station", "Words about the train", and "Words about the seaside". These words would be read through frequently with the teacher, and they would be used for reference as the children wrote stories and diaries. It may be helpful to describe two centres of interest, one with a six-year-old class and one with a seven-year-old class, through which many of these reading activities arose.

3.   *The hospital as a centre of interest with six-year-olds*

Hospital play with these children was more organized than it was with the younger children, and more attention was paid to detail. The interest arose partly because some of the girls were given nurses' uniforms for their birthdays and partly because several children in the class had been in hospital. So it happened that when the girls brought their uniforms to school and put them on in the creative period, there were several children who joined them quite spontaneously in hospital play, using the tops of their tables as beds. When this play persisted for several days the teacher realized that here was an interest that could be developed and used to help the children with their reading.

In a short lesson at the end of one of the creative periods, she discussed the hospital with the whole class. The children decided that they really wanted a hospital in their room. They decided that they would call it "*St. Peter's Children's Hospital*". They would need bandages, sheets for the beds, and bottles for the medicine. The children either brought from home or made all of these things and many more, and soon the hospital play was in full swing. On some mornings it was difficult to find the teacher in this room for she was stretched out on an improvised bed being bandaged by enthusiastic nurses. Boys and girls alike joined in the play. Much reading material arose from the interest. First came the notices, which were put on the wall in the hospital corner. The first three were:

"St. Peter's Children's Hospital"
"Please be very quiet"
"Some children are very ill"

Later others were added. There was one saying:

"Visiting hours, 9.30 to 10.30 every day"

and there was a whole collection of labels to be worn by the "patients" round their necks. On these were written their supposed ailments:

"I have a bad head"
"I have hurt my leg"
"I have a bad arm"
"I have a sore throat"

The nurses and doctors read the label and bandaged or treated the patient in the appropriate way. There was also a box containing medicine bottles and spoons, toy stethoscopes and so on, which was labelled *"Hospital Box"*. The doctors and nurses wore labels as did the ones in the younger class, saying:

"I am a doctor"
"I am a nurse"

and the "Mothers" and "Fathers" from the class next door dressed up in their most elegant clothes came and sat solemnly at some of the bedsides.

A wall story using such an interest would not be difficult to make, although this class did not in fact have one. It could easily have been made on these lines:

"We are making a hospital"
"It is called St. Peter's Children's Hospital"
"We are using our tables as beds"

There was, however, a list of *"Words about our hospital"*. In it were included such words as:

"*Hospital*
"*Doctor*
"*Nurse*
"*Bed*
"*Bandage*
"*Medicine*" and very many others.

The children became familiar with these words, for they were actually reading them in the notices and on the labels in their play each day, and they could begin to use some of them in their news writing.

Simple apparatus for use in the "skills" period was devised using the hospital vocabulary. There were word matching, and simple "reading and doing", cards, using the actual vocabulary of some of the notices:

"Draw and write 'I have a bad arm'"

The child had to write the sentence and then make a drawing showing that he had understood it.

The children borrowed small Wendy House tables from other classes and on these they put vases of flowers, and books for the patients to read. This hospital was such a scene of continuous treatment and strenuous activity, that the patients found little time to read. The interest could, however, have been developed for the quicker readers along these lines. There were several children in the class who could very well have written and illustrated stories to provide material for the patients to read. Many more could have written letters to them. These activities might have extended to other classes, for in the class above this one was a group of children with a lively interest in making story books, and in the class above that was a post office so that letters to the patients could have been posted and delivered. This co-operation would have been quite possible during the creative period, when the children can move freely from room to room.

4. *The Post Office as a centre of interest with seven-year-olds*

The post office began in an interesting way. The class, of which the average age was seven years, had reached a point at which there was no centre of interest in the room. The teacher, thinking that it would give rise to much suitable reading and number work, suggested that they might like to make a draper's shop. The children rejected this suggestion and unanimously decided that they wanted a post office. The next step was to plan what form the post office should take.

The children set to work to make the counter. They painted orange boxes and nailed strips of wood across the top of two of these. They made a grille from wire netting nailed to a framework of wood. They painted red a large, cylindrical, cardboard container from the school kitchen store room to make a pillar box. The children wanted their post office to be a part of a stationer's shop, so another counter was made from which the stationery could be sold. While some children were engaged in these large pieces of construction, others were making the goods for the shop and the post office. They soon built up a large stock of stamps, envelopes and birthday cards. They put the classroom scales into the shop for weighing parcels, a postman's sack was made, and somebody brought from home a postman's hat.

While all of this was going on, a wall story was being written, describing how the post office and shop were being made. These were the first sheets, which the teacher wrote in bold script and the children illustrated:

> *"We have made a counter and a grille"*
> *"We have made another counter"*
> *"We have made some stamps and books of stamps"*
> *"We shall sell birthday cards and envelopes"*

This material was very simple and most of the class could read it without difficulty.

This centre of interest lent itself to the writing of notices. There was the usual label saying:

> *"Our post office"*

and a number of other notices:

> *"You may buy stamps here"*
> *"Post your parcels here"*
> *"Buy saving stamps"*

At the stationer's counter were such notices as:

"We sell birthday cards"
"Large cards 6d."
"Small cards 3d."

After they had begun to use their post office the children thought that they would like to have a telephone. The G.P.O. was most co-operative about this and they installed in the classroom two instruments that really worked, so that it was possible to talk through the instrument from one side of the room to the other. It was fitting that there should be instructions over the telephone, telling the children how to use it. These were printed by the teacher on a large sheet of cardboard, and were as follows:[1]

1.   *"To make a telephone call*
"first lift the receiver
"Next insert four pennies
"Then dial your number
"When you hear a reply
"press Button A and speak"

2.   *"When you make a 'phone call*
"please be brief
"Other people may be waiting
"to use the 'phone"

These instructions were, of necessity, much more difficult to read than the earlier notices, and the slower children needed considerable help with them.

The next development was to learn to send telegrams, and here again there was a notice explaining how this could be done:[2]

"If you have an urgent
"message to send, and
"your friend is not on the
"'phone, you may send
"a telegram.
"3d. for each word"

[1] Note to Second Edition: It should be borne in mind that many parts of Britain have the Subscriber Trunk Dialling system and different instructions will be needed.

[2] Postal and telegraph charges are subject to alteration.

A great wealth of individual work was possible with an interest of this sort. Many of the children wrote letters to their friends in other classes, and the class postman delivered them. There was also apparatus to be used in the skills period. Much of it was apparatus combining work in reading and number. There were, for example, cards with varying numbers of stamps stuck on them which asked the child to:

> "*Buy these stamps*"
> "*Write down how much money*
> "*you spend*"

There were shopping cards for use in the stationer's shop:

> "*Buy a large birthday card*
> "*Buy a small birthday card*
> "*How much have you spent?*"
>   or
> "*How much change have you from 6d.?*"

From this interest, apparatus for children with widely differing standards of attainment could be made.

The post office vocabulary in this class was not written on a sheet to be displayed on the wall, but the sheets were fastened together in a book, which was hung in a place where it was easily available. The children could refer to this when they needed words for their writing. They referred very frequently also to words in their original context in the wall material.

The post office interest provided plenty of reading situations for the abler children. The post office authorities provided literature on the subject, and from these books and pamphlets, pictures were cut. These were stuck into a large book which was called, "*Our book about the post office*". Sentences were written in the book by the children to explain these pictures. For example, there was a picture of a sorting office and underneath was written:

> "*Here you can see the letters being sorted. The letters*
> "*for each town, or for each part of London go into a*
> "*separate section*"

The children gained fresh and interesting information about the sorting, carrying and distributing of mail, and they gathered this knowledge together in a book that they themselves made. Other children who could read fluently went to the children's section of the local library and borrowed simple books about the post office.

In the beginning some of this reading was too difficult for the less able children. They played with the others, but often, in spite of all that the teacher did to prevent this, they were hesitant and lacking in confidence. Then it happened that John, one of the strongest personalities in the class, went to the cinema and saw a Red Indian film. This so fired his imagination that he persuaded many of his friends to go too, and within the space of a few days this group of children who happened to be the most fluent readers in the class, was launched upon an enthusiastic Red Indian project.

The slower children retained their interest in the post office and did so with increasing confidence. The very small group of children who before had attempted nothing more difficult than to read the simple wall story now began to buy and sell, to use the telephone and to try to read the instructions as they did so. The reading material was familiar through having been in the room for a considerable time. They had also ceased to be inhibited by the performance of the quicker children.

Many centres of interest will spring up in a class that has the right amount of freedom. Our skill lies in recognizing them and using them to good effect.

Chapter 13

THE BOOK TABLE

THE book table or book corner that formed a part of the reading environment at the preparatory stage, will continue to do so throughout the Infants' school. In every classroom there should be a well-kept book corner in which there is a good selection of carefully chosen books. At every stage in their school life, both the good readers and the slow readers should be able to go to the book corner and find suitable books to read.

Some teachers like to help the children in their choice, so that the slower readers are not discouraged by taking a book that is far too difficult. Books can be divided into two sections, and marked in a distinctive way. A red spot, for example, can be stuck on to the covers of all the easier books and a blue spot on the harder ones. The children know that generally they read either the "blue" or the "red" books. It often happens that the slower reader is attracted by the cover or the pictures of a book that is too difficult for him. Of course we should let him have the book to look at and talk about. Perhaps he will like to try to read some of it with our assistance. Most of his books, however, should be chosen from the appropriate section.

In the middle classes of the school, most children will have passed through the preparatory period. Their spoken vocabulary will be increasing, and their interests will be widening to include shops, trains, school, pets, and holidays in the country and by the sea. They will like to read simple books on these subjects, and also books that extend their knowledge without departing too far from the familiar.

We can give them books about ships and aeroplanes, books about the animals they may have seen at the Zoo, and simple stories of the everyday adventures of children of their own age. They welcome action in stories, rather than sentences that only describe the object in the picture. Books of nursery rhymes are suitable at this stage as the text will be familiar and the child's confidence will be increased when he finds he can read it. This, too, is the time to introduce some simple picture dictionaries, not only as an aid to writing diaries, but for the child to look at and enjoy. The separate sheets of the wall stories can be fastened together to make a book, and placed on the book table or hung near it.

There is an increasing number of published books available for this stage. When we are choosing them we should look for print that is clear, well-spaced and bold. The pictures should be well drawn and in good colour and the covers strong and attractive. Poorly bound books do not last, and it is difficult to teach children to care for books that fall to pieces after only a very little handling. If we choose books that are suitable in every way except that they are bound with very thin card and have the pages secured with a metal staple, we shall find that they will very quickly get shabby. When this happens they should be removed from the book table and if necessary replaced with new copies. Books of this kind are usually very cheap so that replacing them is not unduly expensive.

We need to take care not to leave them on our book tables when they begin to fall to pieces, for the child may think that it does not matter if all books look like that when he has used them. We should try to help him to take a pride in keeping the books fresh and clean. Transparent polythene jackets in various sizes for slipping over the dust cover of the book, and books in strengthened bindings can be bought. Using these will prolong the outward attractiveness of the book and give it a longer life.

Many books are available for the fluent reader. Children who can read simple stories with little help from the teacher will enjoy reading adventure stories, stories about animals, scripture stories, simple books of reference, books of poems, and some well-known fairy stories. Many of these children will be able to write stories of their own, and they will be delighted to have them put on the book table for other children to read.

We must choose the books for these children with discrimination, remembering that by our choice we shall be helping to mould their taste. The stories, although they are simple, should be well written

The illustrations should be well drawn and the colour good. In choosing books of this quality we shall be doing something to combat the influence of the comics and the poorly written and illustrated books which may be all that the child himself possesses.

For these older children the print need not be so large. The text should, as far as possible, be continuous and not broken up by pictures that make the lines of uneven length and hinder the rhythmic eye movements that the child is beginning to develop as he reads fluently. The stories should be comprehensible in idea. If they contain too many words that the child can pronounce but not understand, he will not really know what the story is about. He will, of course, increase his reading vocabulary by meeting some new words, but the burden of these should not be too heavy. If he cannot read them at all his teacher will help him. If he can pronounce them without understanding their meaning, he will begin to develop the bad habit of "skimming through" a story and not really reading it.

He may be tempted to read in this wrong way because he wants to add a lot of titles to the book list that we encourage him to keep. It is not difficult to discover, by asking questions, whether the child has really read the book. He should not be allowed to write its name in his list of books that he has read, until we are satisfied that the reading has been thorough.

By the time he is transferred to the Junior school the child should have learned to respect books and to care for them. He should have begun to turn to them naturally, as a means of getting information. Most important of all, we hope that he will have learnt to love books, and that he will want to go on reading. The book table, if we have used it rightly, will have played a large part in helping him to develop these good reading habits.

Chapter 14

NATURE INTERESTS

ON the nature table in a class of six-year-olds there will still be the specimens labelled with either a word or a sentence. Many children will have become skilled in the reading and replacing of labels such as these during their first year in school. For some this exercise will still present difficulties. The abler children will now be ready to follow their interest in nature through more difficult reading material.

The teacher and children together can make simple books and write in them facts about specific nature interests. For instance there may be *"The book about our guinea-pig"*, *"The story of our silkworms"*, or *"Our goldfish book"*. In a book about a classroom pet will be information about what he eats, how his box is cleaned, and so on. A book of this kind will be illustrated by the children. *"The story of our silkworms"* may be a record of the children's observations from the time the eggs hatch to the emergence of the moth from the cocoon. Here again, there will be pictures drawn by the children with sentences written underneath.

The sentences may be written either by the teacher or by the children. If the making of the book is a class activity, some short class lessons can be used for this purpose each week. The children decide what they want to say on the new page, and then this can be written by a child or by the teacher. Sometimes only a group of children will be interested and these may like to make individual books.

Six-year-olds can record the growth of plants in more detail. At an earlier stage many children were not ready for more than a simple sentence saying, *"Watch our beans grow"*. Now, they will be interested to put a card behind the plant on which its growth can be recorded. At the bottom of the card can be the sentences:

"Monday. Today we planted our bean"

Above that will be written, a few days later:

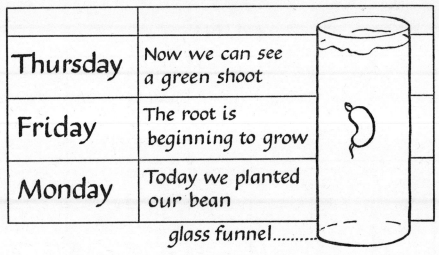

Thursday	Now we can see a green shoot	
Friday	The root is beginning to grow	
Monday	Today we planted our bean	

glass funnel..........

A chart kept by six-year-old children to record the growth of a bean

> "*Friday. The root is beginning to grow*"
> "*Wednesday. Our bean plant is as tall as this*"
> (a mark will be made to show the height of the plant)

The recording of the height and the description of the growth will be continued through several weeks.

In order to maintain the children's interest, especially in town schools where there is not always a readily available supply of specimens, the character of the nature table can be changed from time to time. It is possible, for instance, to have a table of "growing things". On this will be potatoes, onions, carrots, grass seeds, mustard and cress, beans, and anything else that the teacher can find. The children can watch and record the growth of these. At another time there could be a table of flowers and twigs. The teacher who herself is interested in nature study will find many opportunities for varying the work in this way.

With six-year-olds the weather chart, too, will increase in complexity. In one six-year-old class the weather chart was made in the following way. The teacher ruled a large sheet of paper to make a calendar for the month. There were four rows of seven rectangles and each rectangle was approximately 3 inches by 2½ inches. In the top left hand corner

		1 Today it rained	2 Today it was cloudy	3 Today the sun shone	4	5
6	7	8	9	10	11	12
13	14	15	16	17	18	19
20	21	22	23	24	25	26
27	28	29	30			

JUNE

A weather calendar

of each rectangle the teacher wrote the date in Indian ink. She printed the name of the month in bold letters at the top of the sheet. One child each day crossed out yesterday's date by drawing a line diagonally from one corner of the rectangle to the other. He then proceeded to draw and write about the current day's weather.

These monthly sheets served a double purpose. They acted as a calendar so that the children were able to see the date at a glance. They also gave opportunity for the children to develop the skill of expressing themselves in writing. A collection of "words about our weather" could be put near the weather record, so that even the least able children could, with a little help from the teacher, successfully make their day's contribution. A few minutes could be taken to read and comment upon each day's sentence.

Teachers will find their own ways of making interesting weather

In a pond
there were 70
swans. 20 flew
away. How many
left.?

70 - 20 = 50.

25. A 'sum story' made by a seven-year-old child

$$25 \times 2 = 50$$

In one house there were 25 people in an other house there were 25 people. How many altogether?

26. A 'sum story' in which writing and number are closely linked

records. The one described above was valuable in that, while the slower children could, with a little help, join in keeping it, at the same time the ability of good readers could be used to the full.

In the last year in the Infants' school, the reading and writing arising from nature interests will be a continuation of what has been done at the six-year-old stage. In addition, many of the children will, by this time, read well enough to use simple books of reference. They will enjoy trying to use bird books, and flower books, and tree books, and books about the seashore in identifying specimens that are brought. These books can either be kept on the nature table itself or on a bookshelf nearby. This lively and enquiring attitude of mind is one that we should encourage, and seek to develop. It is particularly desirable for this generation to whom information comes too easily through television, films and visual aids of all kinds. Knowledge acquired through the child's own effort in simple research will tend to last, and to be valued by him. When his interest is awakened, he will want to read in order that he may find out more.

One seven-year-old class showed interest of this kind. Their young and enthusiastic teacher was herself deeply interested in nature study and particularly in birds, and the class was quick to catch her enthusiasm. She talked to them about birds and showed them pictures of common birds that they might be likely to see. The classroom was on the first floor, and a look-out post was set up close by one of the windows. In this post were binoculars, and at certain periods during the day groups of children used these to observe carefully the birds that came into the playground or into the neighbouring trees. Also in the look-out post were books for recording what was seen. The children put food on a low roof nearby, so that, even in a built-up area near the centre of London, some birds came close enough for the children to see.

When once they were really interested, these children were ready to receive some quite detailed information about birds and their nests. They learnt about the structure of a bird's wing and were shown carefully prepared examples. They took an old bird's nest to pieces and made a list of all the things that had been used to make it. They went into the local park to look at the birds there, and they began to make their own bird books. Children who were fortunate enough to go into the

K

country at weekends brought back feathers and disused nests, and information about birds that they had seen. They identified specimens by using the reference books on the nature table. They made books into which they stuck pictures of birds or nests that had been brought from home. They wrote in the book about the pictures they had brought. This interest in birds was more planned and organized than the simpler interests of the first year in school, and highly informative in character, as well as providing reading material that was suitable for children with widely varying ability.

This range of ability will also be considered in planning the weather records for a seven-year-old class. For the slower children it may still be desirable to provide some form of permanent chart on which day, date and weather can be changed. Most of the children will be ready for something more varied than this. Many children at this stage enjoy keeping their own weather diary in which they record daily changes. Changes in the direction of the wind, and some effects of these upon the weather, can be observed and recorded. Instead of individual books there can be a large class book in which the children take turns to write. Sometimes a weather diary and a nature diary can be combined. In a book of this kind an entry might read:

> "*Monday, April 4th*
> "*It is sunny today. The weather-cock shows*
> "*that the wind is blowing from the south-west.*
> "*It is a strong wind and the washing on the*
> "*line is blowing about.*
> "*This morning Alan brought some primroses that*
> "*he found in the woods on Saturday. Here is a*
> "*drawing of the primroses*"

Nature interests with older children, even in the town school, should lead the children to explore, to observe and to investigate. They should be able to grow things. They should have opportunities for watching animals and birds, and they should record what they have seen. They should also have facilities for reading books either from the nature table, the book corner, or the public library, so that they may find out more about the living things that they have observed, collected, or grown.

Chapter 15

OTHER READING INTERESTS

THE three most effective ways of approaching reading through interest are through the writing of diaries and stories, through the centre of interest, and through reading and enjoying books. There are, however, other interests that play their part for all or part of the time. The following are some of those which occur most frequently:

1. *Reading arising through number interests*

It is very common for reading to arise in connection with number activities. In some children, a desire to learn to read may be awakened through material of this sort. In playing at shops, for instance, reading and number are very closely connected. In order to be able to buy and sell, the child must be able to read the price-list and the price tickets. If he is not certain about how to give change, he will be helped by being able to read the money chart. If, during the "skills" period, he wants to use the practice shopping cards, he must be able to read such simple sentences as:

> *"Weigh 2 lb. of sweets*
> *"How many are there?"*

These activities may be sufficiently attractive to call forth the effort and interest needed to deal satisfactorily with the reading material.

For older children there will from time to time be measuring activities of all kinds. For some specific purpose the child may have to measure and record the size of furniture in the room, or of boxes to be made into shops and houses. To record the lengths he must be able to read the measuring chart on the wall on which are written the words, "yard", "foot", "inch", "inches".

In the "skills" period there may be practice work in measuring, in the form of a wooden box in which are several partitions. In one section is a tape measure. In another section will be lengths of coloured ribbon, and in others lengths of lace, cord, coloured braid and so on. One section will contain a collection of instruction cards:

> *"Measure the red ribbon*
> *"Measure the green cord*
> *"Measure the blue braid*
> *"Write down how long they are"*

Here again, interest in the activity will help the child to learn the necessary reading material.

Many similar examples may be given. There are children who possess a strong number interest. If we are quick to recognize this interest, and skilful in our planning, we can use it to awaken in the child a desire to learn to read.

2. *Reading arising through the development of the play interests of the preparatory period*

When these activities are carried on into the second year, the reading that accompanies them will increase in difficulty. In one class of six-year-olds there is still a sand-tray. Over the tray is a large notice saying:

> *"We can make these things with sand,*
> *"Castles   Towers   Tunnels*
> *"Ships   Pies   Mounds"*

The teacher has painted pictures of the things that can be made, so that the notice is a most attractive one. On a small adjacent shelf are brightly painted tins containing collections of shells, and large and small coloured paper flags. There is also a collection of cards to be used with the sand. These cards give instructions for the sand play:

> *"Make a big castle*
> *"Put six towers on it*
> *"Put a big flag on each tower"*

In this way reading is organized by the teacher around the children's interest in playing with sand.

In the first year in school there is often a notice by the collection of clay models, which says:

"We have made these things with clay"

There may also be notices on individual models, such as

"David's elephant"

In the second year the children are ready to learn many more words in this connection. In the class in which the sand-play was developed, this widening of reading vocabulary was brought about in the following way. On most mornings during the creative period, models in clay were made. At the end of the period the children put their models on top of a low cupboard. For the slower children there was still a simple notice saying:

"Put your clay models here"

On the wall above the models was a large sheet of manilla card on which the teacher had written:

"We can make these things with clay
"Aeroplanes   Elephants
"Trains   Horses
"Helicopters   Dogs
"Bicycles   Birds"

The list went on to include all the things that were frequently made by the children. Several times a week the children and teacher together would talk about the models that had been made, and try to find their names on the list of words. This list of words was also useful to those children who wanted in their news time to write about what they had made.

Similar examples could be given from most of the classroom activities. Painting is one that lends itself to this development of reading. On the tiles in our corridors we stick large sheets of paper and on these the children love to paint. Children from the three six-year-old classes join in this activity, and labels are fixed above the paintings telling us about them. Sometimes these labels are printed by the teacher. This happened when the children in one class painted very large pictures of people they knew. Over these were written such sentences as:

"Here is all Gordon's family"
"This lady has green stockings"

Children from other classes were attracted by these paintings and wanted to read about them. Other children wrote on their own paintings. Some of this work was really valuable, as children who had made little start in writing their own news were gripped by this painting interest and wanted to write about their paintings. In this way an interest in creative writing began.

3. *Reading arising from an interest in music*

Some children may be helped in beginning to read by an interest in music. In one of our classes there was a music corner. The teacher made a stand, four feet in height, having a four-inch wide shelf on either side, and two feet from the ground. On this shelf were kept percussion band instruments. From the top of one side of the stand was hung a chart on which were pictures of all the percussion instruments with their names. The pictures of the instruments were slotted into the chart so that they could easily be removed. On the other side of the stand hung charts of the scores of the songs that the children knew. These charts had the names of the song written at the top, and at the beginning of each line of notes was a slot for the picture of the instrument that was to play that line. Both the teacher and the class used the stand in their music lesson, and the children used it by themselves in the creative period. They soon learned to read the names of the instruments, and the titles of the songs.

Occasionally children enjoy seeing the words of the songs they are learning. This happened very naturally in one classroom where the children had planted a small garden. They learnt a song about a seed, and the teacher wrote out the words of this song and put them on the wall over the garden. The children sang the song and learnt the words by heart, and even the slowest readers soon began to recognize many of the words. In this way an interest in nature and an enjoyment of singing worked together to help the children to learn to read.

4. *Reading with home-made anthologies*

Children will readily accept the suggestion that they should make books of this sort. They may, for instance, make a collection of "Hymns we know". The teacher will write the hymns on large sheets of paper and the sheets will be joined together to make a book. If the book is made with loose leaves new hymns can be added as the children learn them. The new hymns will be useful reading material for most of the children in the class. The familiar hymns, like the songs in the previous section, because they are known by heart will help to give the less able readers a feeling of confidence as they read them. They will also be available for reference when the children want to know how to spell words as they write their diaries. Many anthologies of this kind can be made. Some that come readily to mind are *"Prayers we can say"*, *"Songs we can sing"*, and *"Poems we like"*.

5. *Reading arising from collections of various sorts*

By the time they reach the top of the Infants' school children begin to enjoy collecting things. This is an impulse that develops at the junior age, but even at the age of seven children like to make collections as a class. In one class where the children were just seven years old, they made a collection of *"Things from other countries"*. A table was set aside for this collection. The teacher covered it carefully with pastel paper so that the exhibits would show to advantage, and as each article was brought, a label was made for it. The children were enthusiastic about adding to the collection, and much reading arose quite naturally from this interest.

In another class, also of seven-year-olds, the collection was of *"Interesting things we have found"*. The parents co-operated in making this collection, and the children brought to school a variety of articles that were difficult to identify. They tried to guess what each exhibit was, and then they labelled it. The labels were not kept in place all the time. They were collected frequently, and then visitors to the room were asked to guess what each thing was.

Another class began to make a collection of *"Things our magnet will pick up"*. Each article that the magnet successfully picked up was labelled. Later a large chart was made saying *"Our magnet picks up these things"*, and underneath were the pins and paper clips and nails, and so on, fixed one below the other under cellophane, and with the name written beside each one.

These are only some of the ways in which reading can be approached through interest at the six- and seven-year-old stages. The advantage of this kind of approach is in that, while it can add to the reading vocabulary of the able reader and lead him to seek information for himself in books, at the same time it can allow the less able child to continue to read informally, with interest, and without any feeling of frustration.

In recent years the Infants' school has been passing through an unsettled period of experiment and change, experiencing both the mistakes and successes that are attendant upon a big forward movement in educational thought and practice. It seems that we have now reached a period of consolidation; a period during which we shall weave all that is best of modern methods into the fabric of our own educational philosophy. No longer are teachers experimenting with revolutionary and unmanageable techniques of teaching. Nor are they providing in their classrooms all the outward trimmings of modern methods with no real understanding of the underlying principles. Rather, there is emerging a method that is neither the old nor the ultra-modern, but which, accepting valuable experience from each, has become a well-considered and balanced policy, expressed in a carefully thought out technique.

Such a method we have considered as it applies to the teaching of reading. Because it has developed as a result of trial and error; because it is based upon an increasing knowledge of children and how they learn and develop; and because it is founded upon practical experience of what is possible for the ordinary teacher with a large class, it is a method which that teacher can practise and develop with understanding and confidence. It is moreover the method which will prove, under existing conditions, to be the most effective.

SOME SUGGESTED BOOKS FOR LIBRARIES AND BOOK CORNERS IN INFANTS' SCHOOLS

THE following list is not intended to be comprehensive. In a field where the number of suitable and attractive books is rapidly increasing the aim (especially in the section for the fluent reader) has been to include a large number of recently published books. In some cases, where a series is suggested, a selection of representative titles is given. Some well-known and suitable books are not included. The reader seeking further information is recommended to such works as *Four to Fourteen* by Kathleen Lines (Cambridge) or to the current book lists of the School Library Association.

PRE-READING BOOKS

E. J. Arnold (Leeds)
NEW COLOUR PHOTO BOOKS S1–12

Blackie
THE WENDY BOOKS 2–12

Bodley Head
Baby Animal ABC
Toy ABC

Chatto & Windus
Jane and Peter Books

Collins
WONDER COLOUR BOOKS
First Things (Colour
    Photographs)

Holmes McDougall
READY, STEADY, RHYTHM READERS
Ready—Stage 1 Red Books
    8 Titles
LET'S READ BOOKS 1–12

Hutchinson
THE DEVONPORT LIBRARY 1–4

Macmillan
PICTURE BOOKS 1–16

McGraw-Hill
JACK AND JILL BOOKS 1–8

Methuen
READY TO READ
METHUEN CAPTION BOOKS
The Red Books 1–4

The Yellow Books 1–4
The Blue Books 1–4
The Green Books 1–4

THE READ IT YOURSELF BOOKS
Set A
Set B

Oliver & Boyd
ANN'S TOYS 1–4
JOHN'S TOYS 1–4
A LOT OF THINGS 1–4

Pergamon Press
OFF TO SCHOOL 1–8

Warne
THE LITTLE PICTURE BOOKS 1–18

Wills & Hepworth
The Ladybird ABC

BOOKS FOR CHILDREN WHO HAVE BEGUN TO READ

E. J. Arnold (Leeds)
EARLY YEARS PICTURE STORIES 2, 3, 4, 6, 7, 8, 9, 10, 11, 12
FIRST STORIES 1–8
SECOND STORIES 1–4
GAY COLOUR BOOKS 1–12

Ernest Benn
FIRST STEPS IN READING 1–4

Charles & Son
THE COLOURED BOXES 1–4

Ginn
TIME FOR READING
The Cherry Family
Penny's Birthday
Penny at School
Story Books 1–12

Hart-Davis
LOOKING AT WORDS 1–12

Holmes McDougal
READY, STEADY, RHYTHM READERS
Steady—Stage 2. Yellow Books 1–5
Rhythm—Stage 3. Green Books 1–4

Longmans Green
READING WITH RHYTHM
Set 1, 2, 3, 4, 5
THIS IS THE WAY I GO 1–6
LETS MAKE SERIES 1–4
READ BY READING
Sets 1, 2, 3

Longmans Young Books
KINDERGARTEN SERIES TITLES 1–17

Methuen
READY TO READ 12 Titles
BRUNA BOOKS 16 Titles

Nisbet
PHOTOGRAPHIC READERS 1–4

Oliver & Boyd
ANIMAL CAPERS 1–3
ROUND & ABOUT BOOKS
TOWN BOOKS 1–4

Pergamon Press
LIVING TOGETHER 1–10

Pitman
LET'S READ ABOUT PEOPLE 1–8
MY COLOUR BOOKS 1–6

Wills & Hepworth
LADYBIRD LEARNING TO READ
BOOKS 2–9

SERIES FOR MORE FLUENT READERS

E. J. Arnold (Leeds)
WE DISCOVER 1–6
SEVEN STORIES OF ROBERT ANDREW
1–7

Burke
OUR WORLD 1–24

Chambers
I WANT TO BE 1–25

Ginn
FIRST INTEREST BOOKS 1–12

Hart-Davis
FIRST FOLK TALES 1–12
ONE TWO THREE AND AWAY 1–4
ONE TWO THREE AND AWAY 5–12
ONE TWO THREE AND AWAY 1a,
 2a, 3a, 4a

Methuen
Mouse Looks for a House
Mouse Looks for a Friend
How Did it Happen?

Muller
JUNIOR TRUE BOOKS 1–50

Max Parrish
Many Foods
Many Homes
All Sorts of Dress
Growing

Pergamon Press
WORLD DOLLS 1–12

BOOKS FOR MORE FLUENT READERS

(In some cases only one title is given for an author or illustrator; readers are advised to look for other titles by the same author or illustrator.)

Abelard-Schuman
by H. Borten
Do You See What I See?
Do You Hear What I Hear?
by F. Shapur
Round and Round and Square

Allen & Unwin
by A. Lamorisse
Trip in a Balloon

Ernest Benn
by E. Beresford
Peter Climbs a Tree
by E. Vreeken
The Boy Who Would Not Say
His Name

Black
by "Aliki"
My Hands
by M. F. Bartlett
Where the Brook Begins
by P. Showers
Find Out by Touching
Follow Your Nose
Your Skin and Mine

Bodley Head
by R. Broomfield
The Twelve Days of Christmas

by C. E. Carryl
A Capital Ship, or, The Walloping
Window-blind
by R. Duvoisin
Two Lonely Ducks
by P. Galdane
The Hare and the Tortoise
The History of Simple Simon
By A. Hewett
Mrs. Mopple's Washing Line
The Tale of the Turnip
by E. J. Keats
Whistle for Willie
by N. Montgomerie
This Little Pig Went to Market
by M. Kornitzer
Mr Fairweather and his Family
by J. Ryan
Captain Pugwash
by R. Sawyer
The Long Christmas
By M. Sendak
Where the Wild Things Are
by W. Stobbs
The Golden Goose
by C. Withers
I Saw a Rocket Walk a Mile
by G. Zion
Dear Dustman
Harry by the Sea
Harry, the Dirty Dog

Brockhampton Press
by L. Berg
Folk Tales for Reading and
Telling

by "Francoise"
Springtime for Jeanne-Marie

by J. Thayer
The Outside Cat

Cape
by J. Burningham
Humbert, Mister Firkin and the Lord Mayor of London

Chatto & Windus
by H. A. Rey
Zozo Takes a Job

Collins
by B. S. De Regniers
May I Bring a Friend?

by Dean Hay
I See a Lot of Things

by D. Maxey
Fidgit

by M. Shulman
Preep

Collins & Harvill
by B. Cerf
Book of Animal Riddles

Dent
by S. Bone and M. Adshead
The Little Boy and his House
The Little Boys and their Boats

Deutsch
by L. Bemelmans
Madeline
Madeline in London

Dobson
by L. Lionni
Swimmy

by P. Smith
Tuning Up

Faber
by V. L. Burton
Mike Mulligan and his Steam Shovel
The Little House

by S. and S. Corrin
Stories for Six-year-olds and Other Young Readers
Stories for Seven-year-olds and Other Young Readers

by R. Hoban
Bedtime for Frances
A Baby Sister for Frances
Bread and Jam for Frances

by B. Ireson
The Faber Book of Nursery Stories

by E. Rose and G. Rose
How St Francis Tamed the Wolf
The Magic Suit
St. George and the Fiery Dragon
The Sorcerer's Apprentice

by D. Ross
The Little Red Engine and the Rocket
The Little Red Engine Goes to be Mended

by J. Townend
A Railway ABC

Gollancz
by S. Hughes
Lucy and Tom's Day

Hamish Hamilton
by R. Briggs
The White Land
Fee Fi Fo Fum

Hutchinson
by J. Chalon
The Story of the Green Bus

Kaye & Ward
by O. Postgate and P. Firmin
Noggin and the Dragon
Nogbad Comes Back

Longmans Green
by G. Clemens
Making Music
Making Sounds
by J. Taylor and T. Ingleby
Number Words
Numbers 0 to 5

Longmans Young Books
by K. Hoskyns and J. Joseph
Boots
Water
Wheels
Wind
by D. Huddy
How Edward Saved St George
by L. Mosheim
A Secret Birthday Present for
  Elizabeth

by A. Thwaite
Jane and Toby Start School
Toby Moves House

Lutterworth
by J. Balet
What Makes an Orchestra

Macmillan
by R. Herrmann
The Christmas Story
The Creation
The Wise Men from the East
by G. Macbeth
Noah's Journey
by R. O. Wiemer
Joseph and His Brothers
Joseph in Egypt

Methuen
by L. Berg
Three Men Went to Work
by D. Bruna
B is for Bear
The Sailor
The School
Tilly and Tessa
by F. Herrmann
The Giant Alexander
The Giant Alexander and the
  Circus
by J. Kruss
Three by Three
by T. Ungerer
The Three Robbers

Nelson

by A. M. Pajot
Galahad the Guinea Pig
Hannibal the Hamster
Let's Grow a Hyacinth
Teresa the Tortoise

Oxford University Press

by V. G. Ambrus
The Three Poor Tailors

by E. Ardizzone
Little Tim and the Brave Sea
    Captain

by J. La Fontaine
The Hare and the Tortoise
The Rich Man and the Shoe-
    maker

by L. Lenski
Davy's Day
The Little Farm
Mother Goose Nursery Rhymes

by W. Papas
Tasso

by B. Wildsmith
Birds
1 2 3

Warne

by L. Weisgard
Whose Little Bird Am I?

Wheaton

by L. Kettelkamp
Flutes, Whistles and Reeds

Whiting & Wheaton

by K. Braun
Kangaroo and Kangaroo

by T. Ungerer
Moon Man

World's Work

by C. N. Bonsall
Who's a Pest?

by R. Bright
Georgie and the Robbers

by P. Spier
The Fox Went Out on a Chilly
    Night

by H. Gramatky
Little Toot on the Thames

by S. Hoff
Who Will Be my Friends?

by C. Johnson
Castles in the Sand

by P. Krasilovsky
The Cow Who Fell in the Canal
The Man Who Didn't Wash his
    Dishes

by J. Langstaff
Frog Went A-courtin'

by A. Lobel
The Bears of the Air
Giant John

by M. O'Neill
Hailstones and Halibut Bones

by S. P. Russell
All Kinds of Legs

by E. Slobodkina
Caps for Sale